A 30-DAY DEVOTIONAL FOR MOMS

RAEMA MAURIELLO

Table of Contents

Introduction

Can we all just agree that no matter the season of parenting we find ourselves in, we don't know what we are doing? No matter how many books we read, podcasts we listen to, pieces of unsolicited advice we receive somehow when we attempt to implement that advice we are met by the spirit of rebellion and then we don't sleep for a month. I have spent far too many hours of my life pretending I know how to stop a child from having a melt down in public. You want to know my secret? I bribed them with cookies. I have attempted to bring four children under the age of seven out to eat together that did NOT have an indoor playground and I left crying. I still haven't figured out how to take pictures with my kids and have them all look in the same direction. I have a child who is driving and it's terrifying (who decided a 16-year-old should be behind the wheel of a car?). I feel like I have lived 18 full lifetimes. I have been a stay-at-home mom, a full-time working mom, a homeschooling mom and I've been a mother longer than I haven't and at the end of the day I have learned: I don't know what I am doing.

Being a mother is not for the faint of heart, we have been knighted to raise, lead, instruct and equip the future generations. Whether we have had physical children, adopted children, maybe you have grandchildren or have spiritual sons and daughters, we have been uniquely wired to love in the deepest and most sacrificial way. We would scale a mountain, fight any giant, and give anything to ensure our kids are healthy and whole.

So, if you are like me, trying to figure it out, this devotional is for you! If you are looking for a how-to guide on being a mother this is NOT the book for you. Within these pages you will read stories of victory but mostly of learning things the hard way and how God has so kindly healed me, forgiven me and brought me back on track time and time again.

More than anything this devotional has been written as a call to arms, to encourage you to stand at your post, to become everything God has created you to be and to draw closer to the Lord. We are fighting battles to try and bring Heaven to Earth in our little corners of the world and need God's grace every minute of every day. For the next 30 days I am praying God meets you right where you are, that your eyes are opened to a new characteristic of who He is, and you fall more in love with Him. So, grab your Bible and journal and open your heart to receive what God wants to speak to you.

Jordan, Dominic, Asher, Brayden, Gabby and me (Raema)

"9-1-1 what's your emergency?"
"Um, I think my house is on fire"

Day 1
FUEGO

December 9th, 2019 I woke up to the sound of a fire alarm chirping, like the battery was dying. Jordan was out of town on a work trip so I quickly went to the fire alarm to remove the battery because I didn't want it to wake up the kids at 2:30am. I would put a new one in when we woke up, I thought. As I stood under the fire alarm I could smell wood burning but it seemed far away like a neighbor was having a bonfire and I could hear what sounded like rain above my head. I walked outside to check if it was raining and it definitely was not. There was no smoke, no signs of flames, and no heat. But something was off. I went to my husband's office on the second floor, the only place I could investigate if there was a fire. I felt the door. It was cool. As soon as I opened the door a wall of smoke filled the room. I immediately closed the door and quickly woke everyone up from a dead sleep, to get them out because our house was on fire. I didn't want to "overreact" but the safety of my kids was more important than my certainty, and my discernment was screaming "get out of the house". I am so thankful that alarm chirped, it never went off again after that, and I believe God made that alarm sound to wake me up.

In this season I believe an alarm is sounding and waking up our spirits. As mothers we need to be especially tuned into what God is speaking and remain sensitive to where He is moving. I think we can become accustomed to the routine of our lives (even if chaos is the routine) and our ears are no longer tuned in to hear the alarms going off.

We have been uniquely equipped, whether you are a grandmother, foster parent, birth mom, stay-at-home mom, working outside of the house, we have all been wired to sense and hear when things are "off." We know the difference between the "I'm hurt" cry and the "I just pooped myself" cry. We know when a child is in distress just by looking at them and we know when they are thriving. It's something God gifted each of us the moment we became a mother.

With the ability to hear the alarms He has also given us the ability to "wake them up" like I had to do to get my kids out of a dangerous situation. I ALMOST took the battery out of that alarm and went back to bed. If I had done that this story would be much different. We can't become deaf to God's warning, His alarms, His leading and His voice. An alarm can sound like a child making threats to hurt themselves (do NOT write this off as them being hormonal). It can sound like words filled with anxiety; it can look like a child sleeping more then normal (which could be an indication of depression). It could look like a new friend group that is leading them to make poor choices. It could look like erratic and violent behavior (which can be an indication of drug use). We can't fall asleep on these cues we MUST take action. It could mean a doctor's visit, a meeting with a counselor or therapist, rehab, homeschooling, and/ or medication.

These kids have been entrusted to US, we are responsible for raising them up in the way they should go, to teach, lead and guide them. We are in a battle for our kids, their future and our lineage and God, in His infinite kindness is equipping us to hear Him in a new way and giving us strategies to combat every plan the enemy has crafted against our families. Numbers 10:9 *"When you go into battle in your own land against an enemy who is oppressing you, sound a blast on the trumpets. Then you will be remembered by the Lord your God and rescued from your enemies."*

Maybe you are in the midst of a situation that seems hopeless and dark; don't allow the pain and the length of the fight to lull you to sleep. Keep you ears open to the alarm and pray like you have never prayed before. Knock on doors, ask questions, stay consistent, and speak up when it's needed. When you find yourself empty and at the end of your own ability, this is where He makes up the difference. Trust that God is leading you even when you don't know what to do.

The whole world seems to be on fire and God is sounding the alarm, do you hear it? Are you moved to action? There is a lost and broken world that can't hear them because they are asleep, God is knighting US to be a part of His story to wake them up.

1. Do you feel like you have been lulled to sleep by the weight of difficult seasons, trials or painful situations?
2. What alarms do you hear going off? (Ex, politics, foster care system, homelessness, sex trafficking, etc.)
3. What part can you play to wake up the sleeping?

Target practice

ONE IN THE CHAMBER

When I served in the Navy we had to stand watch (this is where you are in a position to "protect" and look out for any danger for a 4-hour shift) and we carried a gun should anything happen while we were on watch and needed to defend the ship. Now the gun we carried didn't have a bullet in the chamber, so that meant if we needed to use our weapon there would be a delay in our response because we had to cock the gun first to put a bullet in the chamber. And to be very honest with you, when we stood watch we never anticipated needing to use our weapon so our awareness wasn't as high as it should have been. Then 9/11 happened.

We had been attacked on our soil, the fight was brought close to home and it changed everything. That same day machine guns were mounted to the tops of trucks and the bases were locked down. Additional positions were added to the watches because now threats were not just on the land but also in the air and in the WATER. Now we had to have a bullet in the chamber because there could not be a delay in our response to an attack. Our awareness was heightened and now you were not met with a smile when you tried to get on the ship, you were met with a serious look from a man or woman prepared to protect that ship and the people on it at all costs.

The enemy is no longer attacking from afar; the fight has become very, very personal. He comes to steal, kill and destroy and there is nothing he won't do to accomplish his goal. He is wreaking havoc on our lives and the lives of those around us, breeding terror and hopelessness. We had been walking around in a state of neutrality, seeing all of the horrible things that have been happening in other nations, happening to other families, happening to people we don't know so we throw quick little mindless prayers up to God then go about our day, but now the fight has come here. It hurts, and we are scared, and we are confused and we don't know what to do. Before, when the attack came, we responded AFTER it happened and often times there was a delay in our response, like a gun without a bullet in the chamber. God is saying, you need to be prepared BEFORE the attacks come. You need to pray BEFORE the tragedies hit. You need to be diligent to seek God's face BEFORE the attacks come. You need to be strong in your faith BEFORE it hits close to home. You need to be led by the Holy Spirit NOW so you know His voice and

His leading when chaos surrounds you. You need to have "a bullet in the chamber" so when you see the threat you can hit it, before it hits you.

God is not saying, "Well, you're on your own! Good luck!" He is saying pray. He is saying to read the Word so you know how to fight a battle that is happening all around us that we can't see. He hasn't left us here to fend for ourselves, He has given us weapons to fight back with but just like any warrior, you have to train for battle. You have to practice DAILY the way you will fight when the war rages all around you.

Ephesians 6:10-18 tells us, *"Finally, be strong in the Lord and in his mighty power. Put on the full armor of God, so that you can take your stand against the devil's schemes. For our struggle is not against flesh and blood, but against the rulers, against the authorities, against the powers of this dark world and against the spiritual forces of evil in the heavenly realms.*

Ask God for wisdom, strategies, insight, for eyes to see and ears to hear. When you have God as the commander of the army, YOU CAN'T LOSE. Romans 8:31 says, *"What, then, shall we say in response to these things? If God is for us, who can be against us?"* When you are in the middle of the battle and you are not prepared to fight, that is when you lose hope, that is when you lose joy, and that is when you begin to question whether God even exists. This happens because we weren't prepared. The enemy does NOT FIGHT FAIR. In fact he fights dirty, he hits you where it hurts the most. You can't stop the attacks from coming, but you can be victorious every single time. And every fight you walk through you become stronger, wiser, more surrendered to God, you see miracles happen, you become a walking testimony to those around you.

1. What does your prayer life look like? Do you pray after something happens or are you proactive with your prayer life?
2. Write down the areas you feel like there is a breach and that the enemy is actively attacking.
3. Find scriptures to stand on and declare over your life and the season you are in and passionately pray until you see the breakthrough.

Perm + bangs + uni-brow + sequins + nylons = the coolest 6th grader

HOCKEY PROS AND PERMS

When Dominic was younger we put him in hockey, because I was raised in Minnesota and that is what you do, you play hockey. We were *convinced* he would go really far and excel because he had hockey running through his veins. We watched hockey on TV, took him to a game, bought him jerseys to wear, bought all of the expensive equipment, took him to practice, drove him to games all over the city and thought, "he's going to crush this!" He unfortunately did not crush it. He didn't like getting checked so he quit and my dreams of being a professional hockey mom went down the drain.

Throughout life we can be convinced about things. We can be completely certain a perm was a good idea. No one can tell us Debbie Gibson's Electric Youth perfume wasn't amazing. Our minds were made up that we would marry one of the guys from New Kids On The Block. Or how absolutely cool Treasure Troll earrings were. C-O-N-V-I-N-C-E-D! Then none of that really panned out for me. There are some things we stood on as truth and fact then the bottom fell out and we were left questioning a lot of things. The one thing that we can be absolutely convinced of is that God loves us and nothing can separate us from that love.

Romans 8:37-39 *"No, in all these things we are more than conquerors through him who loved us. For I am convinced that neither death nor life, neither angels nor demons, neither the present nor the future, nor any powers, neither height nor depth, nor anything else in all creation, will be able to separate us from the love of God that is in Christ Jesus our Lord."*

Paul is writing this to the Christians in Rome. He is reminding them that nothing here on earth can separate us from the love of God. Paul calls himself the chief among sinners; he persecuted the Christians then had a miraculous encounter with Jesus, which set him on a path to now proclaim the gospel instead of persecute those who did. He says, "For I am *convinced.*" He experienced the love, grace and mercy of God when He didn't deserve it. He was chosen and called by God when he would have been the least likely candidate but he had an encounter that changed the trajectory of his life and he was CONVINCED that there was nothing, absolutely nothing that could separate us from the love of God.

I think one of the ways to become convinced of His love for us is to actually walk through trials. It's in the pain we see what we are really made of, we see where our abilities end and His continue. We see who is really for us and who isn't. We see the things we have made idols because they burn away in those moments. We see His fingerprint even when we hurt. He shows Himself so faithful even when we aren't. He has been so consistent that I am convinced there is nothing that could separate His love from me, even if that something is me. Even if I try to run or push Him away I can't even separate myself from His love. There is nothing people can say to convince me otherwise, I have too many personal encounters with Him to believe any different. I am CONVINCED! Do not disregard the hard seasons or when things don't go the way we hoped they would, this is normally when we see God operate in the most powerful ways.

Remember back on a time when you cried out to God to rescue you, and He did. When you needed Him to come through and He did. When you needed Him to move a mountain and He did. When He was tangibly present in the middle of trials and chaos. How He makes the wrong things right. If God did it for you then why would He not do it for you now?

You are MORE than a conqueror. When you have the Creator of the Universe on your side, the name that is above every other name at your disposal, you can't lose! God is still writing our stories, but we stand tall, our faith is strengthened, grace is extended, love is fiercely displayed and another win goes to God.

1. What things were you once convinced of that didn't happen the way you hoped they would?
2. How has God revealed his steadfast love to you in the midst of disappointment or pain?
3. How has God shown his love for you even when you didn't "deserve" it?
4. How has being convinced of His love for you transformed your ability to trust in difficult seasons?

Day 4

WHO DO YOU SAY I AM?

If I were to gather five of my friends and asked each of them who I was to them, I would get five different answers. There may be similar answers from each but to each of them I have different experiences and memories. To some I am a friend who they can just sit and laugh with, to some I am the friend who challenges them, to some I am the friend who is a train wreck, to some I am the friend who shows up when they need anything and unfortunately to some I am a friend that hurt them. This would be the same process if we were to poll a group of people and asked them, "Who is Jesus?" You would get a wide range of answers, some would answer from personal experience, some would answer from what they have heard others say and some would answer from head knowledge, things they know but have never experienced.

While Jesus was here on Earth He asked his disciples this same questions. "*Jesus and his disciples went on to the villages around Caesarea Philippi. On the way he asked them, "Who do people say I am?" They replied, "Some say John the Baptist; others say Elijah; and still others, one of the prophets." "But what about you?" he asked. "Who do you say I am?" Peter answered, "You are the Messiah.*" (Mark 8:27-29)

There are two ways to answer the question, "Who do you say I am?" from the head or from the heart. Our head will give facts and statistics but our heart gives personal encounters as examples. Sometimes we can answer this question with some awesome answers, we can pull Biblical definitions from the Old Testament, we can recite quotes from Tozer or Spurgeon, but the most powerful answers are the ones that come from the people who are walking with Jesus.

The longer I live and the more trials I walk through and victories I experience, I add to the definition of who He is to me. And when someone asks me who Jesus is, I get to pull answers from the bottomless well of personal encounters I've had with Him. I get to boast about how He came through for me when no one else did. I get to paint a picture of a Father who accepted me into His family, even though I was rebellious. I get to smile and reflect on the gifts He has given me, while I am so undeserving. I don't have just Biblical definitions of who He is; I have personal experiences no one can take from me. I can boldly stand in front of people and not waver in my stance on being a follower of Christ because He is so much more real to me than this world. I don't fear rejection because I have a friend who will always stand by my side. He is Emmanuel to me.

I believe God is examining our hearts and asking us the same questions. "Who do *YOU* say that I am?" The disciples walked with Jesus, they were close to Him and He looked at them and asked them "Who do YOU say that I am?" He is asking each of us personally this same question, He doesn't want to know what others say, He wants to know what YOU have to say. He wants to know if you trust Him, do you love Him, do you agree with Him, is your hope in Him, is He your source?

He is asking the wandering son and daughter, "Do you believe I will welcome you back home?" He is asking the single mother, "Do you believe I am your provider?" He is asking the broken, "Do you know I can redeem you?" He is asking the rebellious, "Do you know I still love you?" He is asking the world, "Do you know I died for ALL of you?" The world is crying out for answers and looking for them in all of the wrong places but Jesus is standing with arms wide open saying, "You have been rejected, abused, abandoned and hurt by the ways of this world, now, who do you say I am?" He is everything the world promises, but never delivers. He is a God who turns it all around, He has done it for me and He will do it for you!

This needs to be a question we ask ourselves frequently, "Who do I say Jesus is?" This helps reorient our hearts around the truth of who Jesus really is. We can get caught up in arguing about theologies, being divided about things that really don't matter, things that get our attention off of the truth of who He really is and what He is currently doing in our lives personally and around the world.

1. Who has God been to you from season to season?
2. If someone asked you today who you say Jesus is, what would you tell them?
3. How does your perspective of Jesus affect how you interact with Him?

Dominic's new car

THAT'S MY STORY AND I'M STICKING TO IT

The day finally came when our oldest, Dominic, could drive and I couldn't have been any happier. I could finally say "good bye" to those 6 a.m. marching band call times, I could send him to run errands, and I didn't have to drive him to work. It was truly well with my soul. We decided to buy him a car and he sat through the buying process so he understood the amount of money that was being spent on this vehicle so he wouldn't take it for granted because, in the words of OUR parents, "money doesn't grow on trees."

One month. He had the car for one WHOLE month before he mysteriously got a flat tire. We took it into the shop and come to find out, it wasn't just a flat tire, but he bent his tire rod. Naturally, we began asking many questions because one doesn't just bend a tire rod driving responsibly. He "hit a curb going like, 20 MPH" and that is the story he was sticking to. However, the mechanic also had questions because that kind of damage doesn't happen just by hitting a curb. And the mechanic shared with us that it was obvious he had been driving the car like this for a while, long enough for all of the tires to be destroyed that caused thousands of dollars worth of damage.

The mechanic said, "it wouldn't have cost so much if we were able to get the car fixed right when it happened. Since he drove the car in this condition for a while unnecessary damage was caused." My husband is brilliant and is a man of few words, needless to say he said ALL the words in the English language and I think threw a couple of Italian words in there as well. After he was out of the words he could finally have a conversation with our son. He said, "Son, if you had only told us when this happened, instead of trying to hide it, we could have prevented unnecessary damage."

Here is the deal though, how many of us are guilty of this same thing? How many times have we made a poor choice, made a mistake and tried to hide it from God instead of going to Him with our problem and asking Him to help us? Maybe you have felt like He doesn't want to deal with one more of your problems, maybe you have felt like this is a ridiculous situation to need God's help with, maybe you have felt unworthy of His help. And by doing this we can often find ourselves with unnecessary pain or additional problems because we tried to hide from God. Maybe we didn't have great experiences with our earthly parents growing up and they weren't merciful or maybe they didn't extend grace when you needed help and this is being projected onto God. The good news is that God is perfect in all His ways, He is gracious, He is kind, He is forgiving, He is merciful, He is our hope.

After living a long life, David penned these words In Psalm 145:8-9 (NLT), *"The Lord is merciful and compassionate, slow to get angry and filled with unfailing love. The Lord is good to everyone. He showers compassion on all his creation."* David was not perfect, He made some really big mistakes in his lifetime but as he reflected back, this is the last Psalm written by David and I wonder if He was looking back on all of the times God was faithful to him, even when David wasn't faithful to God. Was He reminded of the times He called on God's name and He answered? The times he needed wisdom and God provided? The times he wanted to run but God pulled him close? The times he was afraid but God gave him courage? If we believe the Word of God is true, and this is what is written about Him, we need to change our perspective of God. We need to see Him as a loving Father who wants good things for us. He doesn't want us to live under a cloud of shame, regret, fear and pain. He wants us to live a life that is fruitful, full of joy, and free. If God is merciful and compassionate we need to have peace when we bring our problems to His feet knowing that He is for us and not against us, that He already has a solution prepared to help us. He is waiting on us to call on Him.

1. What problems are you afraid to bring to God?
2. Do you feel unworthy of God's help? If so, why?
3. Reflect back on a time God came to your rescue, and write it down. Thank God for His provision and remind yourself He is the same yesterday, today and forever and He will rescue you from what you are currently facing.

Jordan digging a resting place for Asher's bunny

Day 6

HEART OF A FATHER

Asher and his friends brought home three baby bunnies. They found them by the lake and devised a plan to care for them, and on a rotation of who would keep them and when. Asher quickly became a "mother hen" and watched over them carefully, fed them at the right times and researched how to raise them. After about a week, two of the bunnies died and the kids were devastated. One bunny survived, and for 24 hours Asher cared for that bunny, watched it, held it, loved it but after 24 hours that bunny didn't make it either. This broke Asher's heart, as he held the bunny and cried and all of his hopes of caring, loving and raising a pet were now gone.

Jordan and I suggested burying the bunny and saying good bye to help him to make letting go special. As I walked to the backyard I found a beautiful moment with Asher holding the bunny and crying as Jordan dug a hole, while repeatedly telling Asher, "it's going to be ok." What a beautiful parallel of God's heart towards us when our hearts break.

Throughout our lifetime we will walk through loss and pain. Sometimes it comes unexpectedly and sometimes we are prepared for it but when it comes, it still hurts. We grieve and can be left with a feeling of brokenness. We can feel as if we are standing alone releasing the thing we loved. This can be anything from a relationship, a dream, a job or a person. I am so thankful that when we hurt, God isn't far off, disconnected and uncaring about our pain, you can find Him by our sides whispering to our hearts, "it's going to be ok."

Psalm 34:17-18 (MSG) *"Is anyone crying for help? God is listening, ready to rescue you. If your heart is broken, you'll find God right there; if you're kicked in the gut, he'll help you catch your breath."*

There have been times when the loss has rendered me speechless, when I didn't even know what or how to pray, all I knew was that it hurt in the deepest way. I didn't know how to communicate how I felt to those around me because I wasn't certain they could relate to my pain. The beautiful thing is when people have a hard time understanding God does not. In this verse above it tells us "if your heart is broken, you'll find God right there."

Through painful circumstances I have been forced to change my perspective. Pain tries every time to get us focused on what we don't have, what miracles haven't happened, the pain that is still present, and the emptiness that is still evident.

Psalm 121:1-2 says, *"I lift up my eyes to the mountains—where does my help come from? My help comes from the Lord, the Maker of heaven and earth."*

In seasons of trial and pain we have to look to God, the maker of the heavens and the earth, the supplier of every need, the lifter of our head, the peacemaker, the restorer. He is the One who has our answers and cares deeply for us. God is present even when the horrible happens to us. He is not far removed, He has not forsaken us, He has not forgotten about us. Through every heartbreaking, difficult, seemingly hopeless situation God is still good. I can look back on every pivotal event in my life that could or would have destroyed me, my hope, my focus, my trust, my faith and see that He was present and carried me through all of it.

I'm thankful in the moments when I have felt broken, God was present. When I didn't think I could go on, He gave me the strength to take another step. When I didn't know what to do, God gave me direction. His fingerprint is present even in the moments we think He has left us. His nature is to comfort, heal, love and restore and He has the power and authority to take our broken pieces and create something beautiful from them.

Maybe you are currently in a season where you are grieving and feeling broken. God is present with you; He is by your side and hears your cries. Light comes, joy returns and goodness is going before you. The Father's hand is extended and ready to lead you through and fighting battles on your behalf.

1. What painful situations have you walked through and you can recall how God was present?
2. When you are grieving or feel pain do you run from or to God? If you run FROM Him, what do you run to instead?
3. Memorize Psalm 121:1-2

Day 7

WHEN IT'S TOO MUCH

I have heard people say, "God won't give you more than you can handle" and perhaps a well-meaning person has said these words to you in the middle of your pain. The problem with this phrase is that is nowhere to be found in the Bible. In fact, I would say the opposite is true, God is constantly allowing us to face trials we can't handle. I can't think of one story in the Bible where there isn't an overwhelming trial someone is facing. Something bigger than themselves, their resources, their faith, their knowledge, their strength, their capabilities. From Adam to Jesus and for the rest of our time here on Earth, everyone comes or will come face to face with a trial that is beyond their own strength.

Why would a loving Father allow us to walk through pain too great for us to handle? Is it because He's far removed and unconcerned about us and our pain? Is it because we deserve it? That is what the enemy would lead us to believe. However, I have a different perspective on this. We live in a fallen world, where things break, bad decisions are made, sickness and disease exist, pain is present and humanity encounters these elements in different ways and often times we can be left with the feelings of defeat. God, on the other hand, encounters them in a different way…with victory.

This is tricky though because there seems to be a chasm between how we walk through trials that are beyond our own strength and God's position of victory. How then, do we continue to put one foot in front of the other and not allow these trials to break us?

Grace.

This sounds like a "buzz word" that can be thrown around to explain this gap between our pain and God's victory. However, this is the glue that keeps us together when we feel like we are facing a mountain we can't see the top of and don't even know how to scale it to get to the other side.

Paul tells us in 2 Corinthians 12:9 (NLT) *"… 'My grace is all you need. My power works best in weakness." So now I am glad to boast about my weaknesses, so that the power of Christ can work through me."*

I love this one small phrase, *"My grace is all you need."* When we feel overwhelmed, like we have come up short, out of options, hopeless, scared, frustrated and at the end of ourselves there is a new well we get to tap into that is limitless...God's grace. God is never far removed from us, or our pain. He is right there in the midst of it with us, He is always present. We have a Father in Heaven we get to call on and the One who created everything is on OUR side, ready to fight on our behalf. We also read, *"My power works* ***BEST*** *in weakness."* This is where God gets to shine. I believe we need to do everything we know to do, exhaust all of our options within our own human power but when we come to that place where we don't know what to do or where to turn this is where God's grace come in like a flood and He does what only He can do. And it's in THIS place where we are able to put one foot in front of the other, where we are told to get up and keep going, where we have a peace that surpasses all understanding, where our spirit is encouraged, where our faith is engaged on a new level and God brings us to the other side of this trial where HE gets all of the glory.

If we were able to walk through life being able to handle everything thrown at us on our own, the world around us wouldn't get to see God's work. It's when we come to the end of ourselves that God can step in and do what only HE can do. Matthew 19:26 says, *"With man this is impossible, but with God all things are possible."* When we are in the midst of a situation we genuinely have zero options, zero ideas, zero avenues of solution we don't need to panic or be afraid that this will be the thing that destroys us. This is the perfect moment for us to ask God for His grace to carry us through to the other side. If we could do everything on our own God's kindness, faithfulness, provision, healing power wouldn't get to be on display to a world that is desperately in need of a Savior. We would get to take the credit and the glory but all of the credit and all of the glory belongs to God. I also like to think this is God proving to the enemy over and over again that he doesn't win, that he doesn't have the power but God does.

1. Write down the situations you have felt were too much for you to handle. How did God walk you through to the other side?
2. What areas are weaknesses in your life that you have had to trust God to make up the difference?

LET GOD DO GOD THINGS

For some reason my kids have lost all trust in my ability to keep them alive and their little worlds turning. My oldest is 17, so I have been doing this ONE JOB for 17 years! They have recently started reminding me that they need to eat, they need socks, they need to be at school at a certain time, as if these are new, hot-off-the-press tasks. "OH! You need to EAT?? When did that start?? How are you nine years old and you have never been fed a meal in your lifetime?" And they have started to notify me that we need to leave because they will be late for school… "You can't even tell time! I know when we need to

LEAVE!" When they make me aware of something that I need to do, but have been doing before they were even born. I now say, "Let Mom do mom things!"

I have been so guilty of doing this with God DAILY!! Sometimes I lose my trust in His ability to do "God things." I forget He is the one who spoke EVERYTHING into existence, He is the one who knew me before the very foundations of the earth, He is the author of every detail of my life, He is the keeper of every dream, He is the reason I live and breath and have my being. When things don't go the way I think they should, I will question and doubt. When I don't understand I try to step in and do it my way, because after all my way is clearly the best way. When I get tired of waiting for Him to move I'll try to move it on my own.

God has been in the business of doing God things since…well, all of eternity. It's fascinating if you read through the Old Testament, story after story paints the picture of God's people forgetting what God had done for them and they stopped calling on Him to do what only He could do and some generations forgot about Him all together.

- Noah was the only guy left on all of the earth who was "a righteous man" no one repented, God flooded the earth. (Genesis 6:9)
- Abraham was promised a son, it "took too long" so Abraham and Sarah took matters into their own hands and made things way more complicated then they were supposed to be. (Genesis 16:1-16)

- Moses was on the mountain too long, so the Israelites decided they couldn't wait any longer for a God to worship, so they made their own gods. 3,000 people died that day. (Exodus 32)
- The generation after Joshua *"knew neither the Lord nor what He had done for Israel"* and the land that Joshua's generation fought for, was taken by surrounding nations. (Judges 2:10)
- The people wanted a king to be like all of the nations around them because they rejected God as their leader, so they chose Saul and a curse was now on the people. (1Samuel 8:1-21).

It's so easy for us to read these stories and think, 'why in the WORLD would they question God after they JUST walked through the Red Sea?" "How would people forget to tell their kids about all of the miracles He did for them?" "Why would they want a King when GOD was their leader?" If we look at our own lives, we are no different than any of these people. We forget every day the only reason we woke up is because God let us. We forget the only reason the sun is in the sky is because God told it to be there. The only reason we have a job is because God is our provider. The only reason we have hope is because He sent His Son to die for OUR sins. The only reason we are here is for His glory. We forget that God is ALWAYS doing God things, whether we acknowledge them or not.

We can be so guilty of minimizing who He is and what He can do and IS doing because of our limited understanding and ability to look outside of our current circumstances. We can make the assumption that He needs our help to do His job. Just a friendly reminder… He doesn't need any of our help to do anything. We need HIS help to do EVERYTHING! I know I have been so guilty of trying to "clean myself up" or trying to "work" for His approval, love or salvation. I have removed His grace from my life and try to do it myself and every single time I am left feeling empty and defeated. We need to let God do God things and stop trying to function in a role we have ZERO qualifications to operate in.

Do you need a miracle? Let God do God things
Do you need provision? Let God do God things
Do you need peace? Let God do God things
Do you need comfort? Let God do god things
Do you need hope? Let God do God things
Do you need joy? Let God do God things
Do you need mercy? Let God do God things
Do you need clarity? Let God do God things
Do you need salvation? Let God do God things

We need to get out of His way and place those things at His feet, ask Him to be God in those areas and have the faith to believe His is able to provide. He hasn't brought you this far to just leave you on your own, He isn't going to fall off His throne and He isn't going to look at YOU to do HIS job.

1. What things have you stopped trusting God to do?
2. What things have you taken into your own hands? What complications did that create?
3. When you strive to make things happen, how does that make you feel?
4. Write a list of all of the things you need God to step in and take care of.

SHAMELESS AUDACITY

When my third child, Brayden, was born he had a cleft pallet. When the pediatrician was explaining it to us the words didn't make sense. As I was holding his tiny body they started telling us that reconstructive surgery was necessary and my mind was flooded with questions like: how in the world did this happen? No on in our family has been born with that. How will this impact his future? What does this mean for how we raise him? What are the side effects? Maybe they made a mistake. The joy of having a new baby quickly turned to fear. We believed God could heal him, we prayed for a miracle so he didn't have to have surgery, we had our pastors lay hands on him and declare healing but that wasn't how his healing happened.

I didn't know anything about anything so I went about my life breast feeding him and treating him like there wasn't anything wrong. Sure, when he spit up, it would come out of his nose but he was gaining weight and was happy. Six months went by and it was time for his surgery. We went to the hospital and the surgeon was running through the list of questions and asked, "How has he been eating from the special bottle?" I replied, "I have been nursing him, we haven't been using a special bottle." The look on his face was pure shock. He took Brayden from my arms and shined a light in his mouth and said, "With this kind of deformity he shouldn't be able to nurse at all." He went in for surgery and everything went perfectly. They let us know he would have a speech impediment and need speech therapy and would have a hard time hearing because of the surgery to his ear canal. To this day, he has never seen a speech therapist nor had a speech impediment and he has perfect hearing.

The answer to our prayer looked different than what we prayed for and it didn't come right away. It was a process but I remember I didn't stop praying and believing God was going to do a miracle. We have to be able to pray for things that are yet to come, that we have yet to see and experience. We have to have the strength to stand in the gap for those who cannot stand. We have to know who we are and whom we belong to, we have to know we have a purpose and He has a plan for not just our lives but for our children and the generations after us.

Luke 11:8 says, *"I tell you, even though he will not get up and give you the bread because of friendship, yet because of your shameless audacity he will surely get up and give you as much as you need."*

Sometimes God doesn't answer our prayer right away. A lot of times when we pray there is a gap between request and manifestation of that prayer. It's not because He is cruel and enjoys our pain, it's because He knows things we don't. He sees things from a different perspective, sometimes our hearts aren't ready for what we are asking for, and sometimes He is working on someone else's heart in order to get us what we need. It's in that waiting period where we can become uncomfortable, it's where the doubt creeps in, and it's where fear tries to make its voice heard.

Unwilling to quit when there is silence, when waiting is required, when what we see doesn't line up with God's promises. This is when we need to tap into what lies deep beneath the surface. This is when we knock, and knock and knock some more. This is when we fight to stay in alignment with His word, this is when we pray bold prayer, this is when we dig in our heals and commit to staying the course no matter how long we have to wait for the answer.

When we receive a report that is devastating, when things get hard, when it seems like we have waited a lifetime we can't give up. We do not give room for the enemy to steal kill and destroy. We do not give freedom to the enemy to prowl around like a roaring lion in our families, in our marriages, in our children, in our jobs in our calling, in our health, in our minds.

We may have to get up and carry on through tears, we may have to pray even when we aren't certain, we have to trust when we can't see, we have to hold tightly to the promises that are made to us. We won't be everything we have been designed to be if we live our lives with a victim mentality, like we have been defeated. We are women who are knighted to rise up and have shameless audacity.

When we sat in the waiting room before surgery with Brayden, there was one other family holding their infant. They had fear in their eyes and we felt led to ask them what they were there for. Their child was having open-heart surgery and they were scared. We prayed over them and never saw them again. Perhaps this is why God delayed His answer to our prayers; maybe He needed us to be in that room with that family because He wanted them to know He sees them, loves them and was present with them in the midst of their pain. Do not discount the miracle that happens BECAUSE of your waiting. We had been shameless with our faith and our prayers and I believe it was because of that posture we were able to stand with that family and pray prayers of faith they didn't have within them.

1. What promises has God made to you that you stopped believing in and asking for?
2. What ground has the enemy taken in your life that you need to take back?
3. What miracles have happened in the midst of your waiting?

Me finishing my first half marathon

UPGRADE

At the beginning of 2018 I decided I wanted to challenge myself so I signed up to run a half marathon. I used to run, so this should be "easy." Now, to clarify the farthest I had ever run was three miles so my confidence was grossly exaggerated. During the training process I learned a couple of things: the first is if you have had more than two children you pee your pants, it's a thing so make peace with it and buy a diaper. Second is you have to buy a certain type of running shoe that has been designed for this amount of running. They are not cheap and they are not cute but the upgrade is necessary if you want to run that distance without injuring yourself. I am thankful I made the investment because I was able to train, finish the race, receive my participation medal and then go to IHOP and eat a plate of pancakes.

There have been moments in my life when I needed to make an investment and upgrade but decided against it, which caused me unnecessary pain. After my husband and I went through the pain of infidelity I SHOULD have invested in counseling but I decided bitterness and anger was a road I would rather take. This decision robbed our marriage of peace and healing for YEARS. When my husband felt led to step into a new position at a new company I SHOULD have upgraded my perspective and cheered him on and encouraged him, instead I complained about how "inconvenient" the business building season was and made life hell for both of us. When it was time for me to step back into working outside of the home I SHOULD have had a conversation about changing expectations and what this new season would look like for our family, instead I became frustrated and felt like my job wasn't as important which caused unnecessary arguments and hurt feelings. When my child wasn't thriving in school I should have been brave enough to make the hard decision and pivot to another option, but by not doing so grades suffered, bullying occurred and their mental health was put at risk.

As we navigate through life we have to be willing to make investments and upgrade certain things in order for us to transition from one season to the next without causing injury or even delay. This can be challenging because it means we have to change what is comfortable, we have to give up things we once loved, we have to look at things from a new perspective, we have to be willing to change and our flesh will naturally reject things that make us uncomfortable. Our lives are made up of moments where we grow and mature and what once worked for us five years ago no longer serves us now so we must be willing to upgrade and step into a new way of doing things.

This world we are living in looks different than it did a mere 10 years ago. The things we held in high esteem are now irrelevant. The way we used to raise our kids has shifted and changed and our methods have evolved, they had to. Like the shoes I purchased, sometimes "upgrading" isn't cute. We can hear that word and think of shiny and sparkly but most of the time upgrading means laying down the fancy for the things that will withstand the marathon that is life. In God's kingdom, upgrading means becoming less so He can become more. It means being humble. It means saying "yes" to His way even when it looks contrary to what the world says.

Mark 2:22 says, *"And no one pours new wine into old wineskins. Otherwise, the wine will burst the skins, and both the wine and the wineskins will be ruined. No, they pour new wine into new wineskins."* When this parable was told this would have been a very silly image because everyone knew you don't pour new wine into old wine skins. The audience would have been thinking, "Duh, we all know you don't do that." Interestingly enough Jesus knows people love comfort and control. They love consistency but He was challenging their mindset. This was referencing a new season on the horizon and needed them to be ready to upgrade.

This is still true today. We need to be sensitive in recognizing when something new is happening and being willing to lay down our old way of doing things in order to receive and step into the new things. When we DON'T and we try to do the new thing with an old mindset, old work ethic, old attitude, old prayer life, we won't be able to sustain the weight of the new thing and it will break us. Upgrades are a gift; they are purifying, humbling and remind us our need for the Lord.

1. What old ways does God want you to upgrade? What thoughts, reactions, habits?
2. How has this season changed and what things do you need to change to walk through it in a healthy way?

UNCONVENTIONAL GOD

Raise your hand if you learn things the hard way, do things backwards and yet God still loves you and writes a beautiful story out of your mess. We fall into a category of misfits but I personally believe God enjoys the misfits because we keep things exciting and He is able to take our stories and show the world what He is capable of doing.

My husband and I did everything backwards. We met while stationed together and started dating. I got pregnant after six months of dating, we got engaged and then married the day before he deployed and all of this happened before I turned 21. I was raised knowing that there was an order to how things should go. I should have been married first, and then had a baby. People had their opinions and voiced them without restraint, often times shaming us, and letting us know we didn't do things in the proper order and that this wasn't how God designed things. I carried that weight for a long time. I always felt ill equipped or disqualified to speak into a marriage that was struggling or extend compassion and mercy towards someone who did things "the wrong way". One night my son came into my room upset, feeling lost and purposeless, questioning his existence and bubbling out of my soul came these words, "If there was no you, there would be no me. God blessed me with you; He saved me from the path I was on by giving me you. He did things out of order so my life could get back on the path He designed for it to be on. Your life is a gift to the world to show them that He does things in an unconventional way because He is willing to do what needs to be done to reach His sons and daughters." I had never spoken those words before that very moment and when they left my mouth the chains I felt bound by fell off.

I will no longer stand condemned or ashamed of the way God intervened to save my life because I believe there is someone reading this who secretly feels the same way. Maybe you have been silenced or shamed because of a path you took and it was not in "order." I want you to know you have permission to be free from the chains that are holding you hostage.

If we look at the people God chose in the lineage of Jesus we will see a prostitute (Rahab), a murdered (David), an unwed mother (Mary) and so many more people who have a shady past, made poor choices, did things backward. But God still chose them and even allowed these things to happen in order to bring about His will here on Earth. In fact, the man (Paul) who wrote a majority of the New Testament started as a murder of Christians but God chose HIM to be the one to go out and spread the Gospel! These things did not disqualify them from being used in God's story.

Paul tells us in Romans 5:20-21 (and I like the Message Bible version), *"But sin didn't, and doesn't, have a chance in competition with the aggressive forgiveness we call grace. When it's sin versus grace, grace wins hands down. All sin can do is threaten us with death, and that's the end of it. Grace, because God is putting everything together again through the Messiah, invites us into life—a life that goes on and on and on, world without end."*

In this new cancel culture people are so quick to think they can cancel us from being used by God because they don't like the path God took us down to bring us to where we are now. If they don't like it, it must not be God. I would like to challenge that thinking and say why can't it be God? Why does God have to fit into a clean and tidy box? Is it because when we allow God to be wild and do things in a messy way it makes us uncomfortable because we can't control Him? I DO believe there is a path to healing and restoration we need to walk down, I DO believe there are things He needs to set us free from. I do NOT believe His grace gives us permission to continue making poor choices. But I also know Jesus paid the debt we owed so that we can live whole and free. We aren't rendered unusable because of our past, God uses it all, the good the bad and the ugly for His glory.

1. What has God allowed to happen in your life that would be seen as unconventional?
2. Have you felt shame or unqualified because things didn't happen in "order" or in a way other people think it should have?
3. How has God used your story to encourage others?

THAT ESCALATED QUICKLY

Gabby came rushing into the house one afternoon, she seemed panicked and told me a story of how she scratched herself on a nail at a friend's house. She had a Band-Aid over it, but she still seemed unsettled over it. "Gabby, what's wrong?" Then she tries to casually inquire about needing a tetanus shot and asked how long it took for lockjaw to set in. Seemed a tad dramatic for a scratch and how on earth would she even know about lockjaw? The whole story was she scratched her leg on a nail. Her brother told her she needs to go to the hospital to get a tetanus shot or she would get lockjaw and die in her sleep. Brothers are the best!

This went from zero to 100 pretty quickly. She simply scratched herself then someone planted fear and panic into her mind, thankfully she came to the ones who had accurate information to calm her down and dispel the lie. I think this happens to me weekly but it looks a little different. I can come across an article about the state of our country and believe whatever is written. I can overhear a conversation other parents are having about their kids' education and how they are beginning to scout colleges while their children are in middle school and I believe I must be behind the curve. I can look at other peoples' lives on social media and think I must be living life wrong because I didn't get family pics at a pumpkin patch in matching outfits. When my kids were really small I would hear all of the debates about breast-feeding or bottle feeding and felt like I ruined my child because I couldn't produce breast milk.

I can be guilty of consuming people's opinions as fact, which can cause me to feel unstable, never knowing what is truth and what isn't. It can cause fear, doubt and anxiety because there are roughly 800 different sides to every story…which one is right? This is the battle we face daily, what is truth? Often times we can find ourselves looking for the truth from the wrong sources. We can go to our friends, social media, Internet, the news and more often than not our last resource we look to is the Bible.

2 Timothy 3:16-17 (NLT) tells us, "*All Scripture is inspired by God and is useful to teach us what is true and to make us realize what is wrong in our lives. It corrects us when we are wrong and teaches us to do what is right. God uses it to prepare and equip his people to do every good work.*"

His Word tells us what is true so we can see where we have drifted in our lives, it can correct us and teach us what is right. When we live according to His Word we live lives that are Holy and set apart, we also have peace knowing we are making choices based off of a Kingdom law rather than an earthly one. We need to read the Word for ourselves, study it so we can stand firm when things are dark and uncertain, when things look like the right decision but something seems "off".

Another thing to keep in mind is that what God says is ok for someone else doesn't automatically mean it is ok for you. We not only need to read God's Word we also need to spend time in prayer hearing His direction. You may be looking for direction on whether watching that new TV show is appropriate for your kids to watch, your friends may say it's ok but you have a check about it in your Spirit. You need to listen to that check because your child may be more sensitive to scary things, and over sexualized content may seep deep into their hearts causing unnecessary pain they will need to tackle later in life. Maybe your circle of friends feel at peace about socially drinking but God has not given you peace about it, it could be because He knows you have a tendency to use things to numb pain when life gets hard and this would become a slippery slope for you. Maybe engaging in a debate is ok for some but if you were to participate, hate and division would plant itself deep in your heart.

We need to stay in His Word, stay prayerful in decisions we make (even the small things we don't think are a big deal) and obey. This obedience piece is where things can become tricky because like Maya Angelou said, "Remember, people will judge you by your actions not your intentions. You may have a heart of gold but so does a hard-boiled egg." If the Word says it, we should believe it and commit to allowing it to change us to look more like Jesus and less like the world.

1. What lies have you been fed and believed to be true?
2. How have lies you have believed affected you?
3. What things have others felt were ok but God didn't give you peace about participating in?

Brayden and Asher eating dirt together

KITCHEN SINKS AND CAR LINE

Nothing scares a mother more than when our kids get quiet because we know something is happening that shouldn't be happening and we spring into action to investigate. My two youngest boys shared a room and their room was above the living room. We put them to bed and one hour later we heard the sound of tiny feet running across the floor…then silence. We immediately ran upstairs, opened the door and found one child sitting up in their bed with a smile on their face (which was creepy) then looked at our other son happily jumping in his crib, covered from head to toe in black sharpie marker. We looked back at our other son and noticed his wall and blankets were also covered with sharpie. He hid a sharpie under his pillow, and then once we put them to bed he climbed into his brother's crib and colored him. To this day sharpies are not allowed in the house.

I think the quiet can scare us. I know I would say things like, "I can't wait until the kids go to school and I have some peace and quiet." As soon as I turn my car on the radio turns on, as soon as I sit at my desk I am working, as soon as I get into bed I scroll through Netflix to see if there is a new show I need to watch. Then I would complain about not having the time to spend with God.

This world is loud and distracting and we have become accustomed to filling every quiet moment with noise and activity. Often times we feel empty or depleted, hungry for God crying out to Him and unable to hear His voice. One reason this is happening is because we are often waiting for a booming voice that will shout louder than the world but more often than not, our answers come in the quiet.

1 Kings 19:11-12 *"...Then a great and powerful wind tore the mountains apart and shattered the rocks before the Lord, but the Lord was not in the wind. After the wind there was an earthquake, but the Lord was not in the earthquake. After the earthquake came a fire, but the Lord was not in the fire. And after the fire came a gentle whisper."*

God is capable of shouting, performing miracles and divinely intervening. What He wants is a relationship with us, where we turn everything off and sit quietly with Him, allowing our ears to tune into

His voice and our hearts receptive to what He wants to speak to us. This requires practice and intentionality. Having a dedicated place and time when you spend with the Lord is amazing, but we also go through seasons where that isn't always possible and that is ok. God will meet with us when we make space for Him.

Be intentional and use the time you have. If you find yourself driving a lot, waiting while your child is at practice, sitting in the car line, washing dishes, or folding another load of laundry, take advantage of that time to pray and to talk to God. During these moments is when I have received a download from the Lord; it's also the place where my attitude has shifted from feeling tired and ornery to having the posture of gratitude and peace. There have been times when I have looked at the sink full of dishes and my first thought is "why am I the only human in this house that sees there are dishes sitting in the sink?" Then I will begin aggressively scrubbing dried oatmeal out of a bowl and start thanking God that I even have dishes to clean and a house full of kids who we get to feed and have money to feed them. It might take a minute for my attitude to change but it always does.

As mothers we don't have the luxury of climbing to the top of a mountain to meet with God. He is faithful to meet us when are changing diapers, when we are feeding our babies in the middle of the night, watching our kids play at the park, and hiding from our kids in a closet. I'm currently in a season of life where my kids don't require as much of my time and attention so now I will sit quietly by the hummingbird feeder and God speaks to me there, or when I am gardening. When we make space for Him and quiet our lives to hear Him, He speaks.

1. What things can you cut out to intentionally spend time with the Lord?
2. What things has God spoken to you when you have allowed your life to become quiet?
3. When have you heard God the clearest?

WHAT IN THE MURDER HORNETS IS GOING ON?

Welcome to history ladies! We have lived through a global pandemic. Not to mention the admission of aliens being real, murder hornets, social unrest, forced homeschooling, America being on literal fire, and a presidential election. 2020 did NOT come to play around and I personally did NOT appreciate it. Probably much like you, I thought this was going to be a very short and temporary thing, I did not anticipate it lasting as long as it did. To pass the time I did puzzles, I baked, I threw myself into homeschooling, I ate everything, gained a bunch of weight, then I decided to get back into shape, I gardened, cleaned out my garage, organized closets, wrote this book…literally anything to pass the time.

Eventually I ran out of stuff to watch on TV and things to busy myself with and noticed weird things coming to the surface. Things like "feelings" and "bad habits" and "toxic thinking" that I didn't give permission to make an appearance.

When we are put in positions where everything else is silenced and busyness goes away, the areas of our lives we aren't allowing God to work on or surrendered to Him begin to come to the surface. I can tend to stuff things down and choose work or busyness over allowing God to uproot the unhealthy things and heal me, I would rather work than confront the areas in myself that are NOT a reflection of Christ. I would rather learn how to build the Eiffel Tower than unpack all of my baggage and let God heal me.

Being broken before the Lord isn't pretty. It's not "instagrammable" it's the parts of us we don't want to acknowledge, maybe the parts that even embarrassed us. It's allowing ourselves to be vulnerable and transparent before the One who sees the areas of our lives that we keep hidden away. Becoming free will require wrestling with God. There could be deep-rooted pain we don't know how to get rid of, it could mean reconciling the things that were painful and we don't understand why they happened. It may mean forgiving the unforgivable. It might even mean allowing God to unlock the bondage of being a "victim" on our lives.

In Genesis 32:22-32 we read a story about Jacob on his return back to his homeland and he encounters a man who he wrestles with throughout the night. Jacob wouldn't stop wrestling with this man until he blessed him (v. 26). This man asks Jacob what his name is and says, "Jacob", in verse 28 the man says, *"Your name will no longer be Jacob, but Israel, because you have struggled with God and with humans and have overcome."*

God is not intimidated by your questions, He is not afraid of your feelings, He is not surprised by your brokenness, He doesn't stop loving you if you are mad at Him. He wants you to wrestle with Him because I believe it's through that wrestling He wants to change the names we have called ourselves. Maybe you have called yourself broken, unworthy, hopeless, addict, faithless, uneducated, fat, unqualified, unlovable. God wants to change your name! He wants you to walk upright, free from brokenness, filled with faith, led forth with peace. He wants you to change what you call yourself. You are His daughter, you are chosen, you are favored, blessed, loved, grace filled, chosen, gifted, qualified, capable.

Do not despise your humanity; we all have our stuff we need to deal with. You may feel like you are wrestling and struggling but God sees you and calls you an overcomer. During 2020 I learned a lot about myself. I learned I strive for perfection, I learned I don't like things being out of order, I like having a plan and when that plan doesn't work out I feel shame. I learned I need way more patience with my kids (hello homeschool). I learned I had walls up to keep people out. I learned I try and succeed to feel value. It felt like wave after wave of wrestling matches. All of them I lost, because I needed to. God loves us too much to leave us the way we are, and some of us are limping through life pretending we have it all together but He sees through our act and this is a new season, where He wants us to be free and whole. God can't fix what we fake. Get in the ring, wrestle with Him and allow Him to uproot, heal and restore you.

1. What are some things that have come to the surface during this season?
2. What areas of your life have you pretended to be ok, but you are not ok?
3. What names have you lived by or called yourself? What does God want to change your name to?

Jordan's homecoming, meeting Dominic for the first time

I DIDN'T SIGN UP FOR THIS

When I was 37 weeks pregnant with my first child, Dominic, I went in for a routine check up. I lay on the table as they measured me, and then measured me again and a look of concern appeared on the nurse's face and she told me we needed to do an ultrasound. They discovered my body was no longer making amniotic fluid and the baby was in danger of outgrowing his space and potentially cutting off his blood supply. They needed to induce labor. It was three weeks early, my husband was on deployment and I was all alone. My husband and all of my friends were on that ship and we didn't have family that lived anywhere near us so I was forced to deliver him alone. Two days later I was discharged from the hospital and drove myself home to an empty apartment with a brand new human. I didn't know what I was doing and I felt so overwhelmed.

This was where the seed of resentment was planted. This wasn't the life I had envisioned for myself, this wasn't why I joined the Navy, this wasn't in my plans and yet here I was, 21 years old with a baby and a husband who was deployed. I despised this new reality and I felt like I was being punished. As soon as my husband came home from being gone for eight months, I unleashed a furry on him. I was certain he was to blame for my life unfolding in a manner I didn't sign up for and I treated it like a curse and not a blessing. Fast forward a couple years and we have more children, I am a stay-at-home mom while my husband built his career and the root of resentment grew deeper and the fruit I bore became more toxic.

I was angry, jealous, lonely, felt unheard, unseen and not valued. I was so bitter that this was my life. I was supposed to be an executive somewhere leading a company, calling the shots, traveling and seeing the world but I was at home with four children, living in the car line, sleep deprived, always breaking up a fight, wiping butts, cooking chicken nuggets daily, trying to avoid looking at my stretch marks and not-so-perky boobs while attempting to dodge the landmine of Legos scattered throughout my messy house. Most days when my husband came home I would unload on him, again blaming him for this life. Now a forest of resentment grew, I was a ticking time bomb and no one was safe.

Resentment means bitter indignation at having been treated unfairly. I felt like I had been treated unfairly and someone had to pay. Unfortunately it was directed at those closest to me and it hurt my relationships. Ultimately, the person harboring resentment is the one who suffers most. It's like drinking poison and waiting for the other person to die. It was rotting me from the inside out and I acted like a victim unable to actually see this life I had was actually a gift, not a curse. I had a husband who loved me (In spite of how awful I was to him), I had four healthy children, I had a roof over my head, we always had food to eat, my husband had a good job, we were planted in an amazing church, and I had great friends. As I reflect on that season, it wasn't my husband I resented; I just took it out on him. I resented God. I was angry that I ended up with a life I didn't "want." What's funny now is that He extravagantly blessed me with the life I have. I was too busy pouting about what I didn't have that I didn't stop to acknowledge what I DID have. If I had continued going down the path I was on before I got pregnant and married, I genuinely don't know where I would have ended up but I *do* know it would have been bad.

I didn't trust that God knew what He was doing. I didn't think He had anything good for my life, I didn't have any control and this left me feeling resentful. I allowed what I had "given up" to replay over and over in my mind and it stole my joy and peace. It stole my ability to celebrate because nothing was ever good enough.

Maybe you feel like this. Maybe you are resentful for the life you now live or the season you find yourself in. Maybe you unexpectedly became pregnant which has changed your plans. Maybe you lost a child and you resent God for this pain. Maybe you wanted to be able to stay home with your children but can't because of financial needs and you resent all of the moments you missed. Maybe you are needing to raise your child(ren) alone because the father didn't want the responsibility. And the phrase that echoes in your mind is, "I didn't sign up for this." I want to encourage you, this may not have been the plan you envisioned but what I DO know is, "*For I know the plans I have for you," declares the LORD, "plans to prosper you and not to harm you, plans to give you hope and a future*" (Jeremiah 29:11). While it may be hard to see past right now, be at peace knowing God is writing your story for the future and it is good. God is not punishing you, He is not withholding from you, He is not mad at you. Allow your focus to be on what you DO have, the blessings He HAS given you. Make gratitude a priority because when you focus and glorify loss you will only see and feel loss.

If you find yourself resentful towards a person, choose to forgive and this could include needing to forgive yourself as well. Repent for allowing your heart to harbor unforgiveness. Seek counseling if you need to talk this out with a professional. Do not stay in this place; it is robbing you of joy and peace when God has created a beautiful and fruitful life for you.

1. Do you feel resentful? If so, why?
2. How has resentment impacted or affected your life?
3. What blessings has God given to you? Take an inventory of all of the good things in your life. Make this a practice daily and thank God for each of those things.
4. Ask for forgiveness from those in your life your resentment has hurt.

Day 16

BRUTAL TYRANT

I was a whopping 20 years old when I got pregnant. I was embarrassed to be so young, this wasn't in my plan, and everywhere I went while I was pregnant I was alone because everyone I knew was deployed. Being pregnant made me very insecure and I created this narrative in my mind that everyone was looking at me and judging me. I imagined that people would be whispering about me in stores. I even went to extreme measures to try and hide the pregnancy. I ran miles and worked out to avoid gaining weight, and I didn't eat very little. I didn't go in public often and when I did I wore clothes to hide my pregnancy. I was ashamed of the position I was in. After I had my son and was in public I was often asked how old I was, and when I quietly told them, some people would even make a face of shock or concern which only confirmed what I felt, that I *should* be ashamed.

Shame is different from guilt because guilt says "I did something wrong," shame makes us believe we are wrong to our core. Shame is defined as a painful feeling of humiliation or distress caused by the consciousness of wrong or foolish behavior. Maybe you feel rejected, maybe you had to make a hard decision others didn't approve of, maybe you didn't make the decision you should have, maybe you didn't get the job or promotion you prayed for, maybe you didn't get the degree, maybe you have been trying to live up to unrealistic expectations, maybe you have relapsed, maybe you said something you shouldn't have; and you feel like because of that, you are wrong to your core.

Shame will prevent us from moving forward, it will paralyze us. It will tell us lies that are so easy to believe like; you don't have permission to move forward, you have become disqualified because of decisions you made, you don't deserve peace or freedom from shame and regret, there is nothing better in store for you, you don't deserve that promotion, you will never graduate college, you will be just like your family members, you won't be anything other than an addict, you don't deserve the kid(s) you have.

I really like the picture Romans 8:1-2 paints in the message version because it accurately depicts how shame operates and functions. *"With the arrival of Jesus, the Messiah, that fateful dilemma is resolved. Those who enter into Christ's being-here-for-us no longer have to live under a continuous, low-lying black cloud. A new power is in operation. The Spirit of life in Christ, like a strong wind, has magnificently cleared the air, freeing you from a fated lifetime of brutal tyranny at the hands of sin and death."*

"Low-lying black cloud" is a perfect representation of how shame works. It prevents us from seeing past our shame and covers up any light at the end of the tunnel. And then another phrase "brutal tyranny" is how shame leads. It will tell us what we can do, what we can say or what we must absolutely not say, where we can go, what we can accomplish, and it will demand we pay penance for any discrepancies until we have paid our debt and are worthy of freedom. With shame, that freedom will never come. Shame is not from God, He doesn't use it as a tactic to try and make us act right or get us back in line. In fact, the enemy uses it to steal time and purpose from us.

Jesus has set us free and has aggressively taken back all of our power and authority from the enemy. Because of the work of the cross and the resurrection of Jesus we have the right to stand before God and others shame free. He paid the debt that we owed and we don't owe the enemy any more of our time, peace, freedom, joy, purpose in order to live the life God created us to live. We are humans so we will always make mistakes but God is in the business of redeeming the things we thought we ruined.

If you are feeling like shame is leading your life I want you to look at yourself in the mirror and declare this over yourself, "Shame, you don't own me. I do not give you permission to steal from my life or me any more. (Name) you are human, you make mistakes, you have been forgiven and there is now no condemnation in Christ. You have been fearfully and wonderfully made, your sins have been forgiven as far as the east is from the west, there is a plan and a purpose for my future and I will live free from shame and condemnation."

1. Have you allowed shame to settle in your heart? If so, from what?
2. How does shame impact your life?

FORGIVENESS

Un-forgiveness can act like a tourniquet we place around our heart. We put it there to stop our hearts from hemorrhaging. What begins as a form of protection from pain can end with a piece of our heart dying. That piece that ends up dying is the piece that pumps blood to the other parts of the body, giving it strength to fully heal. We can become calloused and lose our compassion, leaving us feeling empty and bitter.

Un-forgiveness is a form of bondage. It keeps us chained to that event, to those emotions, to those thoughts. It prevents us from moving forward and it acts as a jail cell. We can become intimately familiar with the pain so much so that it acts as another part of our body.

This leads us to live our life as a victim. It's interesting when you speak with someone who is dealing with un-forgiveness or a massive amount of pain because it leaks into conversations; they filter their responses and perspective through the lens of that pain. Un-dealt-with pain and un-forgiveness even affects relationships, decisions and our overall quality of life and we can take the label and lifestyle of a victim which caps our ability to move forward with our lives.

Forgiveness does not mean we forget what has taken place in the past. Forgiveness removes us from acting as judge and jury, a weight we were not created to carry. That is a role for God and God alone. By choosing forgiveness we are giving God permission to act and move as our vindicator and bring justice. What we have the ability to do at times is categorize those who God loves and does not love based on how they have treated us. The fact of the matter is that God loves everyone. It's not "fair," it doesn't make sense but it's the truth. If we were to go off by God's standard of who deserves forgiveness none of us would qualify. That is why we call Jesus our Savior. Luke 19:10 says, *"For the Son of Man came to seek and to save the lost."* I was once lost and very, very undeserving of His forgiveness but He died to set me free too. Our flesh would lead us to believe there is a line in the sand where there are offenses too great to forgive, that we get a "free pass" and some things are just "unforgiveable."

This is NOT the example Jesus set for us to follow. He hung on a cross and one of the last statements He made before He died was, *"Father, forgive them, for they do not know what they are doing."* (Luke 23:34 NIV) Jesus was innocent; He was mocked, beaten, and suffered greatly before He died yet He was more concerned about forgiveness and our eternal position with the Father than His own vindication.

To go one step farther, after Jesus said these words on the cross those standing by watching continued to mock Him. There were two criminals hanging on crosses next to Jesus, who heard Him ask the Father to forgive those who were crucifying Him. One criminal joined in mocking Jesus but I believe because of Jesus' heart posture of forgiveness in the midst of pain and being falsely accused the other criminal recognized Jesus was innocent and undeserving of this punishment. He recognized His response to unfair treatment was unlike anything he had ever seen before, and I believe He saw Jesus for who He was, the Savior who came to set humanity free. The Savior who had been promised and spoken of from the beginning of time, the King of Kings and Lord of Lords, now hung on a cross next to him, asking God for forgiveness for the very people who were crucifying Him. People were sent to the cross to die, Jesus went to the cross to forgive and set people free. Forgiveness is powerful. And because of Jesus' radically different response, the criminal asked Jesus to remember him when He came into His kingdom and Jesus responded, "*truly I tell you, today you will be with me in paradise.*" That man was guilty and he was facing the penalty of his crime but even then Jesus extended mercy and forgiveness towards him. It doesn't make sense and it isn't "fair" within our human understanding but that's how God's economy works.

Like Jesus, when you choose to forgive those who have hurt you, those around you might insult you. They may mock your decision, they may encourage you to hold onto bitterness and try to reopen the wound. But you aren't extending forgiveness for them; you are extending it for you. People don't have to understand it because sometimes it's hard to put into words what God is calling us to do even when we would have every right to be angry and bitter. What if people were watching how you walk through your pain like that criminal was watching Jesus? What if your decision to forgive no matter what causes a ripple effect like it did for that man hanging on the cross? What if your decision to forgive pointed people to Jesus? What if those who are guilty found salvation? It's not such a far-fetched idea because it happened, even as Jesus took some of His last breaths here on Earth. He displayed what impact forgiveness can have, not just here on earth but also in eternity.

1. Are there things that you have not forgiven?
2. How has un-forgiveness affected you mentally, spiritually or even physically?
3. Are there things you have not forgiven yourself for?

Dominic, Gabby, Brayden and Asher hating the diamond mine.

Day 18

FIELD OF DISAPPOINTMENT

For Brayden's birthday we took him to the Diamond Mine in Arkansas. He was convinced he was going to find a massive diamond and become rich. When we arrived he asked us where the caves were and where he would get his helmet and pick axe. He clearly had this picture of what the day would look like and unfortunately reality looked much different. There were no caves or pick axes, instead there was a large flat dirt field, shovels and a lot of hole digging. Based on the general attitude of those who were also digging holes in the field, frustrated parents and crying children, none of us expected this to be how we would be spending our day. Needless to say we were not there very long, we did not find any diamonds, and we will not be returning.

I don't know about you but this story is such a real depiction of how I have approached a lot of my life. I have been known to romanticize upcoming seasons of my life and have been met with a dirt field and a shovel. Getting married was supposed to be nothing but bliss—here is your field and a shovel. I knew having kids wasn't going to be easy but I didn't know it would be THIS hard—here is your field and shovel. Writing books was going to be glamorous and books were going to fly off the shelf—here is your field and shovel. Full time ministry was supposed to be ease, laughter and skipping—here is your field and shovel. This is how life goes though, things don't just happen and it requires a lot of sowing in order to reap a harvest.

There is an interesting verse in Psalm 126:5-6 NLT that says, *"Those who plant in tears will harvest with shouts of joy. They weep as they go to plant their seed, but they sing as they return with the harvest."* I've held this verse close to my heart when life hasn't panned out the way I thought it would, when I have seen more pain than harvest and feel like I have nothing to sow in that season.

What this verse tells us is, when you are in seasons of weeping, you can find hope in a harvest that will come when you continue to faithfully sow. Your sowing may look like helping those in need, staying at your post as a mom, serving in church, giving financially, staying in your marriage, helping to build a business, praying bold prayers....and sometimes sowing is done with tears.

You have to have faith if you want to reap a harvest because it requires sowing. Faith is the ability to sow seeds and trust a harvest is coming, waiting with anticipation even when our eyes have yet to see life spring from the ground. Sometimes it can take years before we will reap what we have sown. I have sown a lot of seeds in the form of tears and I am waiting to see the harvest for but I trust that God is who He says He is.

There is no tear that goes left unseen, no prayer that goes left unheard and no pain that is ignored by our Father. He is the Lord of the Harvest, and He provides seed to the sower, the tricky part is that we don't get to choose the form of seed that is provided but what we DO know is the harvest is always for our good and His glory. Our part is to trust and to sow even if weeping is involved. If we wait for all of the conditions to be perfect before we sow, we will never reap a harvest. We may have dreams in our heart but we will never see them manifested if we wait until the sky is blue and the temperature is warm to step out in faith.

He is faithful, even when we can't see the harvest. Maybe this season is hard for you, but what I do know is God is close to the broken-hearted, you are not alone and you haven't been disqualified from good things because your current seeds are tears. Take what you have and sow them, God promises a harvest of joy. Be patient, fix your eyes on Him and continue to sow, there is a broken world waiting on your harvest so they can have the faith to sow as well.

1. What seeds have you sown? What harvest are you waiting for?
2. What season have you sown seeds in the form of tears?
3. What kind of harvest have you reaped from those seeds?
4. What seeds are you waiting to sow until the conditions are perfect?

HE CHOSE TO SLEEP IN THERE!

We were between houses and my sister-in-law was kind enough to let all six of us stay at her house for a little over a month. Our kids had to share rooms but my oldest was insistent that he have his own space so he decided that he was going to sleep in a closet, that was going to be his and no one was allowed in there. When we were touring houses we would go from room to room and each child would decide which one would be theirs. My oldest found a room that he would claim as his own if we were to buy that house and yelled through the house, "THIS ROOM IS MINE! NOW I DON'T HAVE TO SLEEP IN THE CLOSET!" I immediately looked at the realtor and had to explain the situation so she didn't think we isolated our child and made him sleep in a closet.

Community is absolutely vital for our health as humans, of all of the people who we could think of, Jesus would be the one person who could have walked through His life without community, but He didn't. In fact, He was intentional to BUILD community. When He began His public ministry He called the 12 disciples to join Him because He knew He would need people around Him to accomplish what He was here on earth to do. For three years He did life with these men and many others and in the last few hours of His life He surrounded Himself with community at the last supper.

We read in Matthew 4:1-11 Jesus was alone in the wilderness for 40 days and this is when the enemy showed up to tempt Him. The first line the enemy says to Jesus in verse 3 is, *"if you are the Son of God"* When we are isolated our very identity will be called into question. We will wonder if we are really loved by God, if He really cares or sees us, if He did this to punish us, we will be asked, "If you are a son or daughter of God why would this have happened to you?" When we are alone these things can easily become truth to us because we don't have people who will speak truth over situation and us.

If you have watched any of the National Geographic movies you have seen the lions going after the gazelle herd. One of the tactics a predator will use is to isolate their prey to get them away from their herd which makes them more vulnerable and unable to escape or fight back. This is not a new tactic; the enemy has been using this from the beginning. He knows we are the most vulnerable when he can isolate us, isolation is where we begin to believe his lies, allow depression to set in, our thoughts become deafening, we make poor choices and ultimately deter us from ever healing and becoming everything God has designed us to be.

Dr. Frank T. McAndrew wrote an article in *Psychology Today* about social isolation and states, “Humans are hardwired to interact with others, especially during times of stress. When we go through a trying ordeal alone, a lack of emotional support and friendship can increase our anxiety and hinder our coping ability.”[1]

There have been countless studies done on the negative side effects of people who have been placed in solitary confinement, and isolation has been used as a form of torture. God never designed us to be alone, Genesis 2:18 shows us, *“The LORD God said, “It is not good for the man to be alone. I will make a helper suitable for him.”* This wasn’t just to populate the Earth, this was because Adam wasn’t at his best when he was alone and we have not evolved past this basic human need.

I am at a loss to explain how grateful I am for the community that surrounds me. When we were in trouble or hurting they would jump into action and provide solutions we didn’t know how to fill. The longer I live the more I have come to realize that I need community, it’s not just a nice concept, but it’s vital to our survival. I know I

---

1 https://www.psychologytoday.com/us/blog/out-the-ooze/201611/the-perils-social-isolation

wouldn't be who I am today if it wasn't for the people who I do life with. They have challenged me to be a better person, to do brave things as well as fight for me when I have been too weak to fight for myself.

1. When have you found yourself in isolation? How has it affected you?
2. What kid of community do you have surrounding you and your family?
3. How has community helped you and how have you been able to help those in your community?

Day 20

NIGHTLIGHT

I can vividly recall being woken up by a child in the middle of the night because they were scared. Interestingly enough they never knocked. They would always be standing either at the end of the bed or at eye level and just stare at us until we woke up like some sort of nightmare child. Most of the time we were too tired to perform the whole routine of putting them back in bed and checking for monsters so they would crawl in our bed (and kick me for the remainder of the night), but they could sleep peacefully and felt safe because they were no longer alone in the dark. There is something about the night that heightens our senses. We can become hyper aware of any sound and because we can't see what made the noise, our brains create an image of what could have made a sound like that and we become afraid of things that aren't even there.

Psalm 91:5 says, *"You will not fear the terror of night, nor the arrow that flies by day."*

"The arrow that flies by day" paints the picture of uncertainty and danger that can strike at any moment without us being prepared for it. This kind of fear will put us on edge, creating every "what if" scenario in our minds in an effort to try and "prepare" ourselves for a harmful situation to unfold.

When we feel like we are surrounded by darkness, this is the time when we need to go to God with our concerns instead of allowing our minds to create a scenario that will cause us fear and anxiety. When we panic, we can't hear God's voice leading us. When we are anxious, we have trouble seeing the next steps God wants us to take. However, we have a Father that is welcoming and will allow us to lean into Him when we are feeling afraid or uncertain. When our lives are unfolding in a way we had not planned on or dreamed of, God doesn't leave us to "figure it out" and "deal with it." He doesn't want us to be led by fear, He wants us to live with peace, stand tall, be confident, and share hope with those around us.

One way we helped our kids when they were afraid of the dark was by putting a nightlight in their room. The light gave them the ability to see what was really there instead of being afraid of what they THOUGHT was there. We tend to do a really good job of filling in the blanks when we can't see the whole picture and many times when we fill in those blanks it's not accurate information. When we feel surrounded by darkness, we serve a God who shines light on every dark thing; giving us the ability to see what is REALLY there, not what the enemy wants us to believe is there. He is the one who has the answers we are seeking. He has the solutions we need, and He has the strategies for our next steps. He is the light in the darkness and our peace in times of uncertainty. Instead of running FROM Him, we need to run TO Him.

Be mindful of those you surround yourself with and counsel you seek when you are afraid, feeling anxious or uncertain because they have the ability to push you towards peace or lead you further down that path of fear. Allow God to be your first "go to" when you are feeling this way so He can speak truth where a lie may have been planted, this is what we need to stand on and hold firmly to because God's truth trumps every other word spoken about the situation.

He is our defender, our protector, our savior, and He is faithful. He knows the enemy is out to steal, kill and destroy, but God is our safe haven and we don't need to be gripped by fear. God has already defeated the enemy and any and every plan he has in place to try and destroy us. Fear doesn't have the authority to lead and guide us because God is our very present help in our time of need. He gets the final word and His Word says His plans for our lives are good.

1. What situations have caused you to be afraid? What is real about the scenario and what are lies that you have believed?
2. Look up scriptures that speak truth over your situation and write them down. When you find yourself traveling down the road of "what if," read those verses of life and truth.

Day 21

WE'VE GOT OURSELVES A RUNNER

Jordan and I went on a date one night, which meant we ran to the grocery store. Our oldest was old enough to watch the other three kids for an hour, we communicated and listed out the normal rules while we were gone and one of them was very clearly stated, do not leave the house. Upon our return we were met at the door by our oldest and was notified that Gabby ran away. Now, at that time she was about four years old and we lived out in the country where there were no streetlights and big stretches of nothingness. Jordan and I immediately began to panic, preparing to call the authorities and put together a search party. Our son finally elaborated that he went and got her and carried her home because she wouldn't come home on her own (and I am certain she screamed the entire way back home). Why did she run away you might be wondering? Well, because her brother was "mean to her" so she put on her tiny shoes and left.

I have definitely had my moments when I have wanted to run away from life, and in some moments I have. Things have become too dark, too heavy, and too cruel that running away seemed like a very real option. We can run away from our call, we can run away from God, we can run away from our responsibilities, we can run away from our identity, we can run away from forgiveness, we can run away from healing. Running away appears to have its perks, we feel like we can escape from the pain or the pressures life has thrown at us if we just run away.

Running away can look like becoming disconnected, drinking to numb the pain, eating to satisfy an emptiness, sleeping around to feel comfort, angry outbursts to feel heard, performing to be validated, getting lost in the social media black hole to escape reality. Running away can look like so many different things but what I do know is if you find yourself wanting to run away or are in the middle of running, just know you are in good company.

- Jonah ran away from God's command. (Jonah 1:3)
- Moses ran away because he killed someone. (Exodus 2:11-15)
- Elijah ran away because he was afraid of Jezabel. (1 Kings 19)
- David ran away because his life was in danger. (1 Samuel 20)

- All of the disciples ran away when Jesus was arrested. (Matthew 26:47-56)

What I love about all of these stories is God's faithfulness to meet them in the midst of running and brought them back to where they belonged. They weren't disqualified because they ran, God still used them all to tell His story and make a great impact on humanity. Maybe you find yourself currently trying to run away, and I say "trying" because there isn't a place we can go to escape God. Psalm 139:7-10 tells us, *"Where can I go from your Spirit? Where can I flee from your presence? If I go up to the heavens, you are there; if I make my bed in the depths, you are there. If I rise on the wings of the dawn, if I settle on the far side of the sea, even there your hand will guide me, your right hand will hold me fast."* It's not too late for you to stop. Running is exhausting and you never find peace. We only find our peace when we are safely positioned where God created us to be.

Perhaps you are where you are supposed to be, maybe you were once a runner but God brought you home. We need to now go after those in our life who are trying to escape, much like my son went after his sister. What if we didn't let the people in our life just leave their posts because things got hard? What if we surrounded them, prayed for them, encouraged them and led them back to safety? May we have the same heart that Jesus has for His people. In Matthew 18:12 he shares this parable, *"What do you think? If a man owns a hundred sheep, and one of them wanders away, will he not leave the ninety-nine on the hills and go to look for the one that wandered off?"* We belong to God and He will do whatever He needs to do to bring us back and that may mean He uses us to bring home the lost sons and daughter. My husband and I felt panic and fear when we thought our daughter was gone, our heavenly Father feels even more passionate about His children. He is passionate about YOU.

1. Is there something you are currently trying to run away from? If so, what method are you using to escape?
2. How has "running" affected your life?
3. Is there someone in your life who is running away and you have stood back and allowed them to?

Day 22

CHICKEN NUGGET CHRISTIANITY

I have a child who has a unique relationship with food. As a toddler he hated the feeling of mashed potatoes and would cry when it was put in his tray. He hated having messy hands and would use his hair as a napkin. To this day it takes him nearly a decade to eat the vegetables that are put on his plate and will gag if he has to eat corn. At one point I called my mom crying because I was concerned he wouldn't eat what I made for him and everywhere on the Internet said if your kid doesn't each fruits and vegetables it would stunt their growth and they would grow up to work in the circus. My mom gently said, "just make what he will eat." You know what that was? Chicken nuggets and Mac and cheese. For WEEKS that is all he would eat. I would sneak other foods in the cheese and slowly introduce healthy food. Some days it was a battle but he needed to eat things that would keep him healthy.

Did you know that our spiritual lives could look like this as well? We can try to live a "chicken nugget Christian" life where all we consume is the stuff that gives us no spiritual depth or truth. We can know fun Bible trivia facts, we can know the stories of the Bible characters and we can stick to just living by a gospel of grace but we don't also receive the message of holiness or repentance. Everyone loves the message of Grace, it's so important to our faith. HOWEVER Jesus also speaks about carrying your cross, crucifying your flesh, serving above being served, REJOICING in persecution. Jesus doesn't want us to just know about it, He commanded us to LIVE these truths. We read about Adam and Eve, about Abraham, Moses, David and Goliath, Jesus, Peter, Paul but are we seeing the truths that we can cling to from their victories AND their losses, or do we just know the information so we can say we read the Bible? "*For the word of God is alive and powerful. It is sharper than the sharpest two-edged sword, cutting between soul and spirit, between joint and marrow. It exposes our innermost thoughts and desires.*" (Hebrews 4:12) The Bible isn't just for us to read and check our "holy" box, its job is to expose our very sin nature so we can repent before a merciful Father and we can change and transform because of the exposure.

We get really good at living under grace, knowing that when we mess up there is grace and forgiveness but at some point we have to stop going back to that behavior and using "grace" as a crutch and we need to start pursing a life of holiness. Being able to live a life of holiness comes from a place of repentance and repentance acknowledges before God, that we are sinners in need of a savior and this is the posture where we invite Him to become more in our lives and we become less.

We can allow ourselves to accept half truths or cherry pick the Bible verses that make us feel good about ourselves and pretend the other scriptures that bring correction don't exist. This leaves us living shallow Christian lives, making us ineffective for the Kingdom. God needs us to grow up, we can't stay baby Christians forever. He needs a body of believers who are willing to do the hard work to continually surrender our lives to Christ, to uproot the unhealthy destructive behaviors, to have self control, to have humility, to be extravagant in our forgiveness, to live a life worthy of our call. We are walking billboards to the world of God's redemptive power, and often times we are just throwing Bible trivia facts at them or an unbalanced message of the gospel that results in zero lasting change. How can we be obedient to the mandate Jesus gave us to *"make disciples of all nations"* (Matthew 28:19) if we aren't willing to be His disciples first. Jesus all but sucker punched the disciples in the face with His message, not because He was mean or heartless but because He LOVED them and wanted them to live lives that glorified the Father and that took a LOT of correction and redirection. When Jesus first called them to follow Him their flesh was in control of their lives not Christ so He had to rewire them to have a Kingdom perspective not a worldly perspective.

This is a process. It doesn't happen overnight and I am most certainly a work in progress. If someone asked an audience to raise their hand if they are a hot, sloppy mess I would be the first one to raise my hand because I recognize I am nothing without Jesus. But I want to take Him as the entire package not just the parts I like. When I would pray this beautiful prayer, *"Search me, God, and know my heart; test me and know my anxious thoughts."* (Psalm 139:23) You know what happened? ALL HELL WOULD BREAK LOOSE IN MY LIFE! He takes that "test me" part seriously and that is exactly what He does. He will show us areas in our lives where our roots are shallow or nonexistent if we let Him. Not because He is punishing us, but because He wants to grow us and mature us into His disciples and this is a lifelong process. We will NOT arrive while we are here on Earth but we should continue to strive to remove the ungodly areas in our lives.

We need to exchange our "chicken nugget Christianity" for the real "meat and vegetables" of the faith, the things that will keep us strong and sustain us until Jesus calls us home. Jesus NEVER promised that being a Christian would be easy. In fact, He promised trials. But we need to have roots that go deep so when the trials DO surface we can withstand the storm. This takes a lot of self-evaluation and honesty about where you are in your relationship with Jesus.

1. Do you allow the words in the Bible to be your guide or just the parts that promise prosperity?
2. How do you act in public? Is it entirely different in private?

EVERYTHING SMELLS LIKE URINE

When we were teaching one of our boys how to potty train, I wouldn't say he "got it" for a while. Once the diaper was off anything that could hold liquid was fair game to pee in so we had to watch him carefully. We got so used to the smell of urine because that seemed to be the scented candle of our life for about two years, that we actually became nose blind to it. It took my mom coming into town, walking into our house and immediately asking us what that smell was for us to investigate. We eventually found he had peed into his Lego bucket, and I am not quite sure how long it had been there so we just threw the whole thing away.

You know what is a lot like this? Sin. I know, kind of aggressive right?

Romans 8:7-8 (NLT) "For the sinful nature is always hostile to God. It never did obey God's laws, and it never will. That's why those who are still under the control of their sinful nature can never please God."

Let's just call a spade a spade. Often times we want to make that word sound less staby, but anything that is an idol, behaviors and decisions that are contrary to God's Word, is sin. We want to sugarcoat the behaviors, decisions and lifestyles that are contrary to God's Word and will for our life, we will allow them to go unchecked because it's "not that bad." Sin that goes unchecked is like chicken pushed to the back of the fridge you forget about, it begins to rot, smell and after a while we become blind to it.

Here is why having accountability in your life, and real honest friends who are cheerleaders for you but will also lovingly shine a light on your sin, is so important. Those are the people who can sniff out your life and say "what is that smell?" Once it's identified we have to be humble and surrender enough to get rid of it. Not to say that it is always that easy, but we are being held responsible for getting it out of our lives.

Unfortunately we live in a culture that has become very casual with sin, because if you can imagine it, it's available to you. We are setting the stage for our kids to grow up in a world that doesn't have the fear of the Lord and doesn't have a passionate pursuit for holiness.

The enemy has done an amazing job painting holiness as boring and no longer relevant but this couldn't be farther from the truth, holiness is the pursuit God has called us to. In Thessalonians 4:7 (ESV) we are told, *"For God has not called us for impurity, but in holiness."* This is a lifelong pursuit to become more and more like Christ by living in this way we will be set apart and the world will be able to see a difference in the way that we live as opposed to how they live.

Sin may be fun for a short while, God knows I spent a whole lot of time choosing sin over God's way, but we will reap the painful benefits of living our lives this way. When we stop pursuing holiness it will cause a separation between us and God and over time we become insensitive to what is God's way and what is the way of this world. We were created for so much more than the foolishness this world provides us. Choosing holiness may require saying goodbye to toxic friendships, you may need to change your daily habits so reading the Word becomes a priority. Maybe you need to start going to church or go back to church, maybe you need to pray in a new way.

If sin has become an easy choice, then you need to get aggressive with killing that desire in your heart. Jesus tells us in Matthew 5:6, *"Blessed are those who hunger and thirst for righteousness, for they will be filled."* If the sinful things of this world are what you are filling yourself up on you will always be left feeling hungry and never satisfied. But when we hunger and thirst for God's ways we will never go hungry or left feeling empty.

The enemy is aggressive with how he tires to get us to choose sin over holiness so we need to be aggressive with how we deal with the sin in our own lives.

1. What habits or lifestyles do you have that are causing you to drift from the Lord?
2. What are areas in your life for which you have become "nose blind"?
3. Who are the people with whom you trust to be honest and vulnerable? Reach out to them and ask them to be a part of you letting go of harmful habits, toxic thinking, or sinful tendencies, and ask them to hold you accountable.

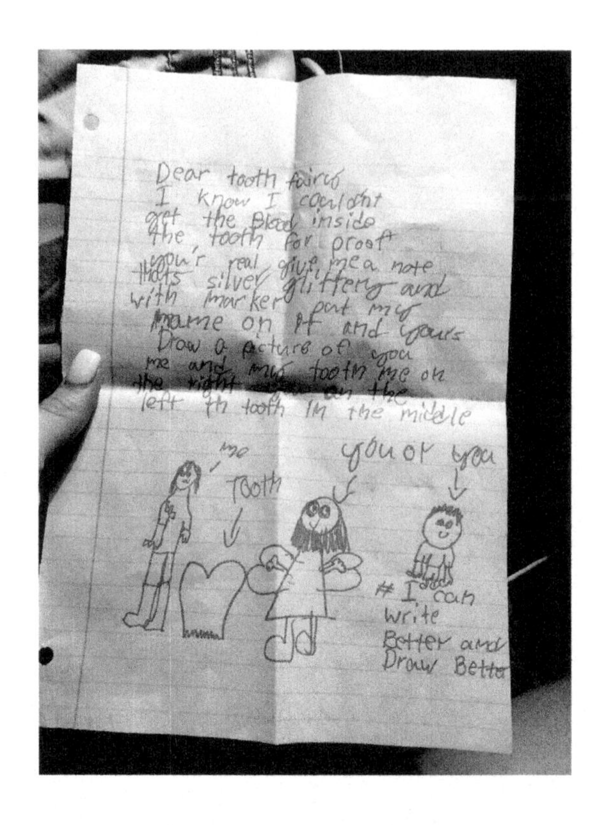

Dear tooth fairio
I know I couldnt
get the Blood inside
the tooth for proof
you'r real give me a note
thats silver glittery and
with marker put my
name on it and yours
Draw a picture of you
me and my tooth me on
the right [illegible] on the
left th tooth in the middle

me
Tooth
you or you
I can
write
Better and
Draw Betta

Gabby's Challenge (Above) My response (below)

CHALLENGE ACCEPTED

Gabby was our last child who believed in the tooth fairy. She was having a hard time believing that this magical being was not real. Santa? Fake. Easter Bunny? Fake. There was something about the tooth fairy that she teetered between believing and not believing. She lost a tooth one day and put it under her pillow. My husband went into her room to exchange a quarter for her tooth but to his surprise he found a note TO the tooth fairy. He brought it into me and said, "This is all you." As I read the note it was a challenge to prove the tooth fairy was in fact who she said she was. A list of very specific demands were listed and I am definitely NOT going to be shown up by a 9-year-old so I got out my glitter paint, my sharpie and my scissors. I completed all of the demands and placed the note back under her pillow. She woke up and came out of her room yelling, "She is real! See!" and she showed everyone in the house the proof. She was so convinced she even brought it to school to show all of her friends who told her the tooth fairy wasn't real.

Her innocent faith inspired me and made me wonder "do I have this same kind of faith when it comes to the Lord?" I would have to say my answer is no. I have faith in the Lord but not this kind. I know the relationship I have with Him is real, I know I trust Him, I know I have seen Him move mountains for us but beyond that, I don't believe I have "child like" faith. I don't know that I have the full ability to throw all caution to the wind and believe God for the absolute impossible. I will often times pray what my brain can comprehend and imagine happening, but I don't find myself believing for the things beyond my own ability.

John 14:12-14 (NIV) "*Very truly I tell you, whoever believes in me will do the works I have been doing, and they will do even greater things than these, because I am going to the Father. And I will do whatever you ask in my name, so that the Father may be glorified in the Son. You may ask me for anything in my name, and I will do it.*"

We could read verses like this and think this kind of access is reserved for those who maybe work in the church, do ministry full time, have never made a mistake, and were basically born saved.

However, I love the word that was not mistakenly placed in this scripture He says the word "whoever." This word literally means, any person. Hard stop. It doesn't list people who are disqualified; it says "whoever believes in me." This is great news for a person like me who needs God's grace daily, seems to only learn lessons the hard way, has a mouth on them, has a long way to go, is the least likely to be chosen for the "holy" award, but this verse includes us too.

Often times my faith is dictated by how "worthy" I feel of God's grace or presence based on my behavior. I will feel bold and ask for big things when I have checked all of the boxes in my brain that would qualify me as a "good Christian" and I will feel like I don't have permission to ask for big things if I didn't do big things. It doesn't work like that, If God's Word says it, then we have access to it. We need to have the faith like a child. Kids will believe (for the most part) anything you tell them. If you say it, it's truth to them and why would they doubt it because they trust you. We need to trust God like this and ask for the big and "impossible" things because God has given us the authority and ability to call on His name and He goes into action.

1. Do you feel disqualified to pray for certain things? If so, which ones and why?
2. Do you trust that God is who He says He is and that you have access to the things the Bible says?
3. What prayer requests do you have that you have been ashamed or afraid to ask for?

THE GIFT THAT KEEPS ON GIVING

I love giving gifts. It's something I look forward to with holidays and birthdays. I enjoy finding things that are unique and thoughtful, I like finding wrapping paper and then giving the gift to the recipients. I think we accidentally started a new tradition for Christmas where we will take one child at a time and allow them to "buy" presents for their siblings. It's always interesting to watch them look for and choose the gift. Two of my children fight and argue with each other as if that was the reason they were created, so when I took them shopping I immediately thought they wouldn't put much thought into the gift that would be given to that sibling. I was wrong. They both knew what they were interested in, what they would enjoy and even made thoughtful comments about why they would like the gift chosen. Watching them wrap the gift and become excited about giving it was really beautiful to watch, never once commenting on what they wanted instead. They were focused on what they were giving.

After my child excitedly left the room with an arm full of gifts to put under the tree the Lord began to speak to my heart. I felt Him say, "The joy you feel watching them give gifts to one another is how I feel when I watch you give your gifts to each other." I know it sounds cliché, but we were genuine created with unique gifts and talents that were placed there not just for ourselves but to give away.

"Each of you should use whatever gift you have received to serve others, as faithful stewards of God's grace in its various forms." (1 Peter 4:10)

Do not compare what you can do with what you see on social media or those who are celebrated publicly. I have friends who have the gift to sing and when they do it actually blesses me. I have friends who have the gift of hospitality and I love being the recipient of it. I have friends who have the gift to love people really well and they have loved me through some really ugly situations. I have friends who can bake, some who can sow, some who are phenomenal home schoolers, some who can organize, some who can act and dance, some who can paint, some who can take stunning photos and some who have the gift of making money.

When I watch them do what God has gifted them to do, I don't feel like I need to compete or prove that I also have something to bring to the table. I actually cry (weird response I know). I feel blessed that I get to be on the other end of something the creator of the universe uniquely grafted into their very DNA. When we withhold our gifts from the world we are left with a gap. Our lives are more beautiful and full when we use what God has blessed us with to love the world around us. I think the fear of failure can prevent us from using the gifts we have but what if we shifted our perspective from being afraid of failing to seeing the people God wants to reach on the other side of us using our gifts. We shouldn't use them in pursuit of fame or applause, rather we should use them to display God's love for His sons and daughters.

I had no idea how to write books but I knew it was something God has wired me to do so I simply Googled how to write and publish a book, then I took the baby steps to make it happen. That is how I published my first devotional *"Because Crack is Illegal.* Unfortunately I delayed in writing this very book for years because I was afraid it wouldn't "do well" and that I would become a one-hit-wonder. I was more concerned with my pride and I lost sight of you, the reader. I forgot there were mothers who needed to hear what I was supposed to share with them. So here I am, still not knowing what I am doing but stepping out and being obedient because it is what I have been gifted to do.

So, what is it that God has gifted *you* to do? Step out, what do you have to lose? And if you need a cheerleader and someone who believes in you, you have me, and God. If I can write books you can do whatever it is God has gifted you to do! The last thing we want to do is get to the end of our lives regretting we didn't use every single gift and talent God put inside each of us to serve others.

1. What can you do this week to begin baby steps towards using your gifts?
2. Who are the people God wants to reach through your gift?
3. How would using your gift bless you and those around you?

Gabby and I get our ears pierced.

Day 26

I'LL GO FIRST

For years I asked Gabby if she wanted to get her ears pierced and her answer was always "no". Until one day, right after her ninth birthday she asked ME when she could get her ears pierced. I immediately looked for the nearest jewelry store that would pierce her ears and we made an appointment. When we got to the store Gabby began to look at the items that would be used to pierce her ears, then she started asking questions about pain, if there would be blood, will she be awake when they do it, and how long does it hurt? It was something she wanted to do but was scared. Since I had mine pierced for roughly 100 years I wanted to get a second hole pierced and thought this would be an amazing opportunity for her to see how it's done to ease any fear or anxiety about the process. She watched intently and looked for my reaction to see if it would in fact hurt. After I was done she climbed in the chair, held my hand and bravely got her ears pierced.

In that moment, someone needed to go first. It was something she wanted to do but she needed someone to show her how it was done and lead the way. We can all relate to this, we will have a dream or goal but we have looked to others who have gone first and accomplished what we want to do as a source of hope and inspiration. We can be paralyzed with fear or uncertainty because we have never seen it done before and we need someone to go first. I have intentionally surrounded myself with women and men who are trail blazers, who are innovators, and who are hill takers. It is a constant reminder that what God has put in my heart to do is possible because I have them as my example.

Before Moses died he commissioned Joshua to take his place to lead the people into the promise land. He told the people in Deuteronomy 31:3, *"The Lord your God himself will cross over ahead of you. He will destroy these nations before you, and you will take possession of their land. Joshua also will cross over ahead of you, as the Lord said."* The people crossing into this land that God had set aside for them had never done anything like this before. They were either slaves, wandering in a desert or born to slaves so they have never lived a life of peace and promises realized. Now was the time for them to step into their inheritance, it was something they wanted but they needed to be shown how to do it.

What if you are being called to go first? What if God wants you to be the first person in your family to stay married and break a generational cycle? What if you are supposed to start a business and by doing so others would have the courage to chase their dream too? What if you are supposed to write the book because lives are on the other side of it? What if you are supposed to put your name in the hat for that promotion? What if it's you who is supposed to pioneer and innovate? It's easy to use the excuse that we are waiting to accomplish what God has placed inside of us because we have never seen it done before, but Joshua had never lead roughly one million people into the promised land but he accepted the responsibility and said "yes." What I love in that verse above is that God was actually the one who went first and Joshua followed His lead.

Going first requires a consistent "yes" to each step God is calling us to take. It's not easy, sometimes it's lonely, sometimes it requires sacrifice, sometimes it means saying "no" to things so you can say "yes" to the right things, sometimes it means doing it afraid, sometimes it means making mistakes, sometimes it means needing to be fluid and ready to pivot. You are created to be a leader; you have the ability to do the hard things that others are afraid to do. You have been anointed and positioned for such a time as this. There is a broken world looking for someone to go first and hold their hand and encourage them to follow your lead.

1. Who is in your life that you are looking to, to encourage and inspire you to do brave things?
2. What things have you been too afraid to start, stop or complete?
3. What is God calling you to go first in?

THANKFUL FOR YOUR "NO"

I almost left our church. Something very, very small hurt my feelings. I never said anything so it sat there in my heart festering until it became offense. My thoughts about the leaders drifted from honor to anger, I entertained toxic conversation, I caused division and it brought me to a place where I didn't want to show up anymore on Sundays. I wanted to leave because "surely there is something better."

After weeks of coming home and crying I finally told my husband "I can't go back anymore. I don't want this to be our church anymore." He gently listened then looked me in the eyes and said, "no." This was definitely not the answer I wanted to hear. I wanted to hear, "you are right, this is hard we should go" but he didn't. He went on to say, "This is where we are called and we need to work through this because leaving would be out of alignment with where God has planted us."

In that season I had surrounded myself with people who felt and thought the same way I did and they celebrated my "bravery" for potentially leaving. I look back on the answer my husband gave and I am thankful for his "no." I am thankful I had someone who was strong enough to say the hard things that I needed to hear. I am thankful he didn't make a decision based on his feelings but based on his obedience to God. We all need a person like this in our lives. We are human and our feelings get hurt or we hear something incorrectly and create a narrative that is not accurate. We can make decisions based on our feelings that can get us off course or stepping out of God's will for our lives and we need some people bold enough to tell us "no."

This could be anything from leaving a job we were meant to be in, ending a friendship we are meant to be in, moving when we are supposed to stay, picking up the bottle when we need to be sober. Having people in your corner who will pray for you, cry with you, fight battles you aren't strong enough to fight, willing to say the hard things, challenge your way of thinking, is so important. During that season I distanced myself from those friends who would challenge my heart posture and my decisions and it took me down a very dark path mentally and emotionally. I now know how vital it is to be intentional with who I have in my inner circle because I almost walked away from my calling. Proverbs 27:6 tells us, *"Wounds from a friend can be trusted, but an enemy multiplies kisses."* Saying the hard things and hearing the truth can be painful but when it comes from someone who loves us and wants to see us become everything God has created us to be it's actually a blessing.

The "kisses" from an enemy will sound like flattery, they will come in the form of alliances, they will have the tone of "us" again "them", and they will sound like truth but have a selfish motive. Be prayerful when you are hurting and those who you allow to speak into your life because deceit can take on the form of "a listening ear."

Today I would say I have more people in my life that will easily tell me "no" than people who will tell me what my flesh wants to hear and it has made me a stronger person. It's not only important to have those people in our world but for us to be that person in someone else's world. Telling someone the truth in love can be hard, especially if we want to please everyone around us. This life is too short to have shallow relationships where we feel like we are walking on eggshells around them and afraid to tell the truth. We need to have a deep love for those around us that we are willing to say the hard things because there is greatness inside of them and we want to do our part to protect them from getting off course.

Have the hard conversations, humble yourself to hear the hard things, surround yourself with people who will fight to protect your calling and thankful for the "no's."

1. What situations do you wish someone had said "no"? What pain would it have prevented?
2. What people do you have in your life you trust to tell you "no"?
3. Do you find it difficult to hear "no" from those around you? If so, why?

Jordan and I baptizing Ricki

LEAVE THEM BETTER THAN YOU FOUND THEM

Her name was Ricki and it was only by God's grace that we met. My husband hired her husband and we had dinner together one evening to talk about the company and to welcome them to Texas. At the time she was only six months pregnant with their fifth child. One month later, we received a call that she had a seizure and was rushed to the hospital where she flat lined, they did an emergency C-section because they discovered she had a brain tumor and they needed to remove the tumor immediately. This began an almost two-year journey fight with brain cancer.

My heart was broken because I didn't want to lose another friend to cancer, as I was praying for her I heard the Lord clearly speak to my heart and said, "Leave her life better than how you found it." Their family quickly became our family. We celebrated kids' birthdays and holidays together and just spent time together. One day she asked me if I would baptize her and this is one of the greatest honors of my life that she would allow me to be a part of such a big day.

Thanksgiving day, 2018 Ricki went home to be with Jesus. She was a fighter, she was hilarious, and she was an amazing mother and an even better wife. She was inspiring. My prayer is that I was able to add to her life and make it better because I know for a fact she left me better than she found me.

I believe this is a lifestyle God is asking from all of us, to live in such a way that we leave people better than when we found them. The Apostle Paul tells us in Philippians 2:3-4 (NIV) *"Do nothing out of selfish ambition or vain conceit. Rather, in humility value others above yourselves, not looking to your own interests but each of you to the interests of the others."*

This verse does NOT mean we need to become a doormat and be taken advantage of but it DOES mean living a life poured out and serving those we encounter. At times this can mean correcting with love, speaking the truth when others in their world are only telling them what they want to hear, sitting with them when they are hurting, forgiving quickly, asking them the hard questions, holding them accountable, fanning the flame in them, and pushing them to be everything God has created them to be. This could also mean something as simple as being kind to the cashier at the store or not yelling at people in traffic.

When we live our lives without vain ambition we aren't doing things to be celebrated or recognized for how we love and serve. It can be really easy to slip into the mindset that we are doing things to end up on someone's social media or being thanked publicly. I know I have been guilty of doing things based on whether I would be seen doing it. That's actually a really exhausting way to live, always deciding whether to do the right thing based on public recognition and celebration for doing it.

We have the honor of being the hands and feet of Jesus to the people we come in contact with, for some people we may be the only encounter with Jesus they will have. Are we living in such a way when we speak they hear His voice and acting in such a way they are experiencing God's goodness when they come in contact with us? Are we honoring others above ourselves or is our agenda to get what we want out of them instead of asking God what He wants to bring to them through us?

Living in this way requires for us to become less so Jesus can become more in our lives which will in turn impact those we encounter day to day and throughout our lifetime. The day we surrendered our lives to the Lord is the day we signed up to no longer live for our selfish desires and ourselves but to live a life poured out to glorify God. A life that is beautiful, at times painful, full of joy and infused with purpose, we make a lasting impression on those around us and leave them better than we found them.

1. How have you impacted the lives of those you have come into contact with?
2. How have you been the hands and feet of Jesus to the people you encounter?
3. Write down five ways you can be a blessing to people this week.

THE GOD WHO SEES YOU

Asher got to be in the Middle School play *The Little Mermaid.* He was so excited; he played a couple of different roles as an extra and was a background singer in different scenes. There is one background character he played in particular that was comical and not meant to be a main character. He was a snail, set on the side of the stage, he didn't say one line but my eyes were fixed on him as if he was the main character in that scene.

Being a mother, we can often feel like we are playing the role of the snail. At times we can feel unseen, playing a part where we don't have a voice, set in the background. It can leave us feeling like the part we play isn't important, less valuable than those around us and unnecessary. When our hearts break, when we need to hear we matter, when we feel alone our cries don't escape the ears of God and we can't escape the eyes of God. When you feel forgotten about by the world and you would like a high-five to acknowledge your hard work, just know God sees you. His eyes are fixed on you, giving a standing ovation for every role you play, a Father proud of His daughter.

There is a story in Genesis 16 of a woman named Hagar. She was pregnant and not treated well by those she was in the care of, so she ran away. As she sat in the desert, alone, feeling unloved and unseen she was visited by an angel of the Lord. God met her in the midst of her pain, He heard her and He saw her. After this encounter Genesis 16:13 says, *'"She gave this name to the Lord who spoke to her: 'You are the God who sees me,' for she said, "I have now seen the One who sees me."'"* Hagar had a unique role to play in God's story and He wanted her to know that she and her child had purpose and value.

God met her in a desert. What is your "desert"? Is it hiding in a closet from your children as you eat old Halloween candy? Is it sitting in the car in the driveway gathering your patience before going inside? Is it folding the 8,769,453 pile of laundry of the week? Is it driving home alone after dropping a child off at college? Is it sitting in a hospital room holding your child's hand praying for a miracle? I believe God will meet mothers right where they are because He knows we don't have the luxury of leaving our post. I remember the late nights feeding each child wondering when I would sleep again. I remember the countless hours sitting in my car picking up each child from school. I remember trying to comfort my child after surgery. I remember every time I had to leave work to pick up a sick child from school. I remember the countless tears I shed out of frustration and fear. I remember needing to allow my children to make the wrong choice and feeling the pain of the consequences. God was there with me, every time. He saw me, He sat with me, and He was present in the midst of all of it.

When we feel weak He is right there to remind us we are strong. When we feel defeated He is right there telling us that we are more than conquerors. When we feel broken He is right there ensuring us He is near to the brokenhearted. When we are feeling afraid He tells us He has not given us a spirit of fear but of power, love and a sound mind. When we don't know what to do He is there leading and guiding us. When things look hopeless and lifeless He reminds us He is in the business of bringing things back to life.

He is the God who sees us, right where we are. He's not ashamed of us, He's not angry when we find ourselves in the desert. He's not disappointed when we feel like the snail. Like Hagar, He has chosen each of us to play a leading role in His story. He has created us with a unique strength to raise up the next generation.

He knows every dream in your heart and knows every hair on your head, He knows every need you have, He hears every prayer you pray and the ones you don't. He is FOR you. You are not unnecessary, you are not forgotten, and you are not voiceless. You have the attention of the creator of the heavens and the earth, you have the ear of the very one who created sound, you have access to the One who sits on the throne and is ruler over all. He is the God who sees you.

1. In what ways do you feel as if you are unseen?
2. Where is your "desert"?
3. What lies do you believe about your role and position as a mother?
4. Write down scriptures about who God says you are and speak those truths over yourself.

TR—STAMP

One night as I was cooking dinner Gabby came into the kitchen holding a temporary butterfly tattoo and proudly asks, “Mom, can you put this on my back like yours?” She turned around and showed me the part on her lower back she wanted it placed. Have you ever immediately regretted a decision YEARS after you made it? That is exactly the feeling I had in that moment. Why did I think getting a lower back tattoo was a good idea? I mean, I know I was only 23 but STILL! This was one of those moments that illuminated how closely our kids watch us and how they look to us to set the example for them. They are sponges and they absorb EVERYTHING...especially the “fun” words you might use while stuck in traffic, they REALLY love repeating those words.

One of the greatest responsibilities we have is not building an empire, but raising the future leaders of the world. We are entrusted with these kids to equip them to build on the foundation we have laid for them. As I was reading through the book of 2 Kings I noticed a fascinating pattern that emerged around chapter 13. In many cases we learned who the king was, his MOTHER'S name, then it said whether he did good or evil in the sight of the Lord. Very few times are women named in the Bible, but this was a significant enough detail to put the mother's names in these accounts.

At times we can feel as though our roles are insignificant and go unseen but the opposite is true. We carry a weight of training up our children in the way they should go and I believe in the sight of God, this is one of the most precious and valuable jobs. How do we ensure we are instructing, loving and leading them well? We need to first be leaned into God…DAILY. This is not a job we can do on autopilot because every day there seems to be a new challenge we get to tackle.

I have faced situations where I have zero idea how to handle it. I have had conversations that I didn't know what to say. I have had to solve problems I never dreamed I would have to solve. I have felt crushed by the weight of this responsibility and I have felt like I was drowning, I have cried myself to sleep and screamed in pillows. The ONLY thing that I could do was cry out to God in those moments. I have to ask Him to give me clarity, wisdom, creative ideas, strength, boldness, peace...and the list goes on and on. And He never ceases to meet me where I am and fill in the gaps where I fall short.

We have to be intentional to share with our kids how God has been faithful to us, how He has rescued us, how He laid His life down for us. We can't shield our kids from all of the hard things life throws at us; they need to see God's hand turning ashes into beauty. We need to bring them along on the journey with us, pointing out the fingerprint of God in every season.

"He commanded our ancestors to teach them to their children, so the next generation might know them—even the children not yet born— and they in turn will teach their own children. So each generation should set its hope anew on God, not forgetting his glorious miracles and obeying his commands. Then they will not be like their ancestors—stubborn, rebellious, and unfaithful, refusing to give their hearts to God." (Psalm 78:5-8 NLT)

There were generations after the Red Sea was parted, the Jericho walls fell, and the Promised Land was obtained who didn't know about God because the generation before was too busy building and conquering. Far be it from us to remain silent when it comes to sharing God's goodness and faithfulness with our kids. May they learn from us how to pray, worship, lead and love the way Jesus would. Does this guarantee that our kids won't drift? Unfortunately, no. Our job is to point them to Jesus, be faithful with the time we have with them, stay diligent and pray for them and then trust that God will do what He does.

1. What stories of God's faithfulness can you share with your kids?
2. What things will you be more mindful and intentional to do in front of your kids set healthy examples?
3. Have you seen your role as a mother as insignificant?

*I do want to acknowledge the role of a father is also important and extremely valuable. I am not insinuating raising children is solely a mother's job.

I don't know much, but what I do know is that there is a war that has been waged against this next generation. It appears as if the enemy is throwing every weapon he has formed at them and not many seem to be bothered by that. We have been knighted as the ones who are responsible for raising up the next generation to lead the way, to be the voice for the voiceless, to fight battles and break cycles so they don't have to, to love deeply and direct wisely. Being a mother is no small insignificant responsibility; it is one of the greatest responsibilities we could ever be entrusted with. We aren't simply responsible for keeping them alive (which some days that feels like all I am doing), we are responsible for raising men and women who will be equipped and empowered to change the world. You may very well be raising the next President, Supreme Court Justice, lawyer, doctor, nurse, business leader, church leader, musician, author, inventor, or social justice warrior.

We aren't here to just get our kids to 18 and send them off, we are here to ensure the kingdom of God continues to be pushed forward, that lost sons and daughters will hear about a God who loves them and has more for their lives, to change the trajectory of the world. One of the saddest verses in the Bible can be found in Judges 2:10 (NIV), *"After that whole generation had been gathered to their ancestors, another generation grew up who knew neither the Lord nor what he had done for Israel."* This is the generation that came after Joshua, the same Joshua who led the Israelites into the Promiseland, the same Joshua who walked on dry ground through the middle of the Red Sea, the same Joshua who walked through the Jordan River on dry ground, the same Joshua who led the battle when the walls of Jericho miraculously fell down. With all of those signs, wonders and redemption the people forgot to train up the next generation and share with them everything God had done for them. The generation grew up not knowing the God of all creation the way just one generation before them did.

Far be it from us to not train, lead and guide this next generation. May we not have a generation after us who doesn't know the goodness and the fear of the Lord. He has been too faithful, kind, generous, strong, forgiving and gracious for us to NOT teach our children about Him. At the end of the day, they aren't even ours, they belong to HIM and we get to be stewards of His creation. What a weighty and noble honor we have been entrusted with.

I want to encourage you, you have been hand selected to be the mother of your child(ren), He has given you everything you need to train them up in the way He has designed them to go. God has placed you and them here because you and they are an answer to a problem in this world. You are strong and capable. It doesn't matter where you come from or what your past handed you, what matters is that you are known, loved and seen by the God of all creation and He has good things in store for your life. In order for us to lead well we need to ensure our own walk with God is healthy because we can't pour from an empty vessel and if we are leading without God leading us we are only teaching from head knowledge not from relationship and head knowledge can easily be forgotten.

Maybe you don't really know about this God I have talked about throughout this book and that's ok, because He knows you. Your past mistakes and failures don't disqualify you from knowing Him in a personal way. He sent Jesus so we would have unlimited access to Him, He loves us so much, knowing we will fall short and willingly choose to do the wrong thing at times, that He sent His one and only Son to pay for our sins because He knew we would never be able to pay penance or do enough "good things" to get to spend eternity with Him. If you want to surrender your life to Jesus or maybe at one point you have but you have slipped away and you want to let Him take the rightful place on the throne of your heart. Maybe you are thinking "I don't want my life to be about me anymore I want it to be about Jesus I want you to say these words below out loud."

> "Dear Jesus I ask you,
> to forgive me, of all my sins
> I admit, I've made mistakes but today,
> I give you my heart I give you my life
> Give me the power, to live for you
> in Jesus name. Amen."

If you said that, I want to celebrate you and say welcome home. God has amazing things in store for you and your family. He is for you, not against you, He has a plan and a purpose for you. Everyday make the decision to allow God to lead and guide you. I still don't know what I am doing, but I am thankful that I get to serve and follow a God who does.

Raema Mauriello is a native of Minnesota and currently lives in Lucas, Texas.

Raema met her husband Jordan while serving in the U.S. Navy and they have been married since 2003. They have four children: Dominic, Asher, Brayden and Gabby.

She is a graduate of Liberty University with a Bachelor's Degree in Religious Studies and continues to work in ministry. She started her career as a Navy Journalist and a Search and Rescue Swimmer and is the author of the devotionals, *Because Crack is Illegal* and *The Struggle is Real.*

Raema is passionate about encouraging and inspiring people to be who God has created them to be and to do what they have been created to do. You can follow Raema on her social media platforms as well as her website www.raemam.com

Made in the USA
Middletown, DE
24 April 2021

38127299R00096